Yanni Voices

T0085025

ISBN 978-1-4234-8452-3

SEVEN PEAKS MUSIC
SEVEN SUMMITS MUSIC

DISTRIBUTED BY

HAL•LEONARD®
CORPORATION

7777 W. BLUEMOUND RD. P.O. BOX 13819 MILWAUKEE, WI 53213

In Australia Contact:
Hal Leonard Australia Pty. Ltd.
4 Lentara Court
Cheltenham, Victoria, 3192 Australia
Email: ausadmin@halleonard.com.au

Visit Hal Leonard Online at
www.halleonard.com

OMAGGIO

Music by YANNI
Lyrics by NATHAN PACHECO

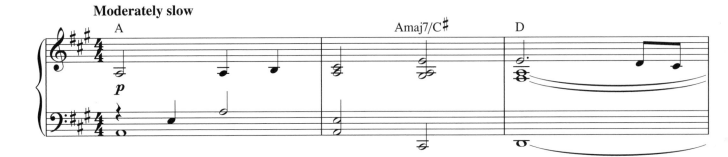

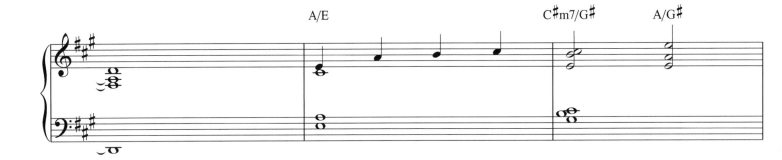

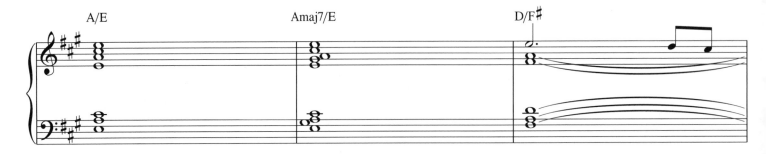

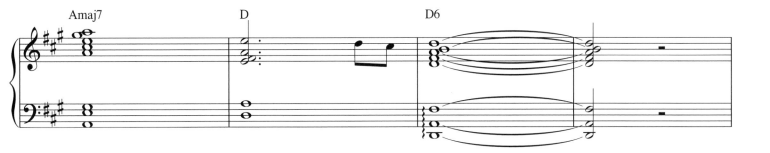

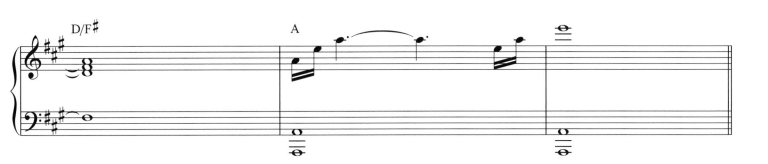

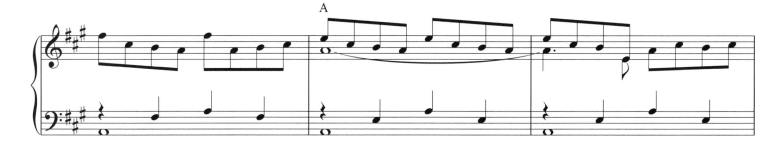

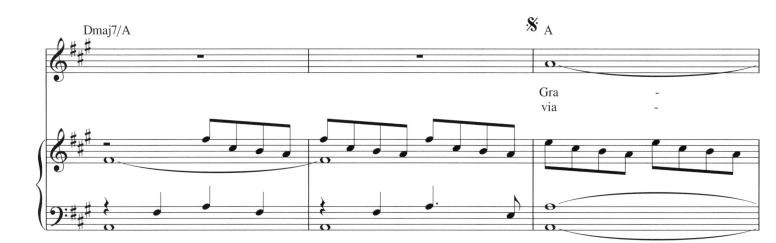

Gra -
via -

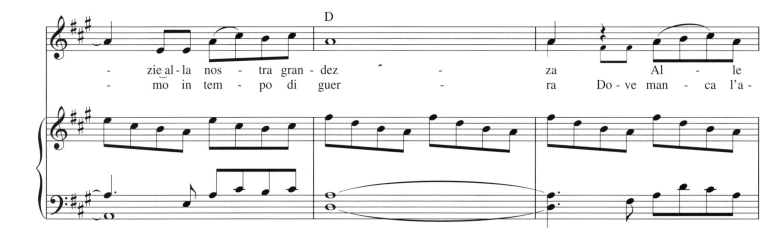

- zie al - la nos - tra gran - dez - za Al - le
- mo in tem - po di guer - ra Do - ve man - ca l'a-

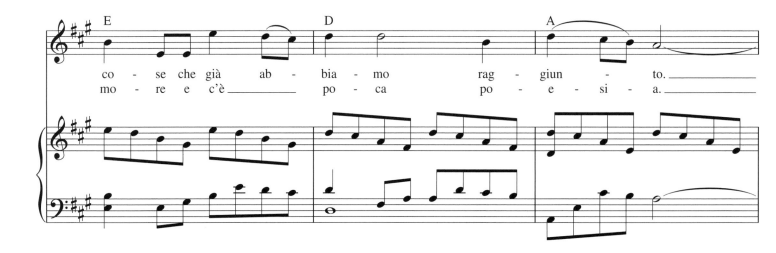

co - se che già ab - bia - mo rag - giun - to.
mo - re e c'è po - ca po - e - si - a.

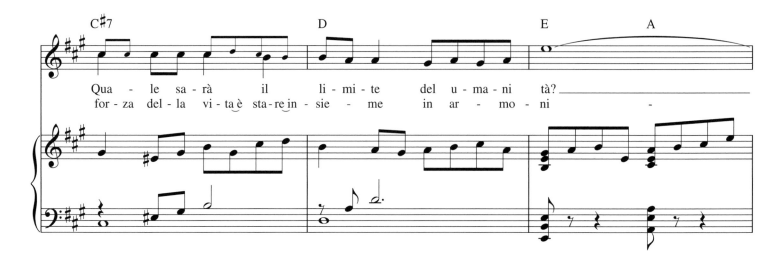

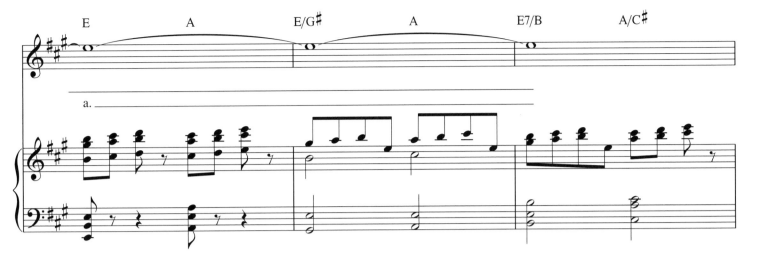

Nien - te è co - si lon - ta - no: i so - gni so - no re - al - tà.

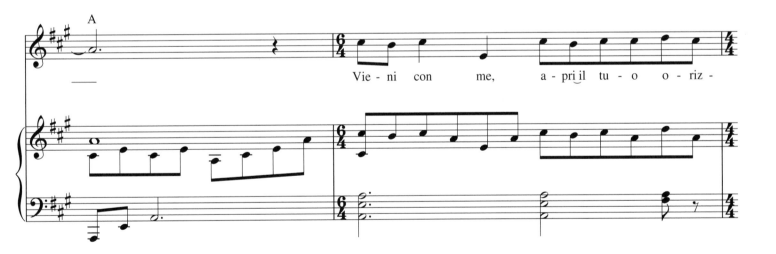

Vie - ni con me, a - pri il tu - o o - riz -

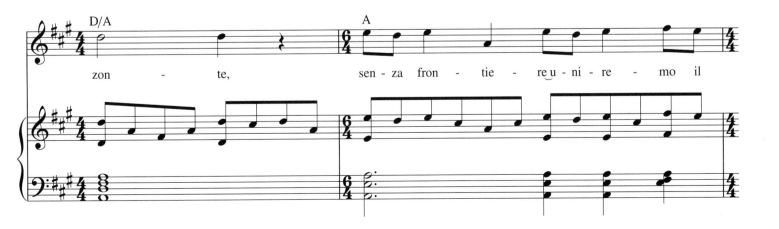

zon - te, sen - za fron - tie - re u - ni - re - mo il

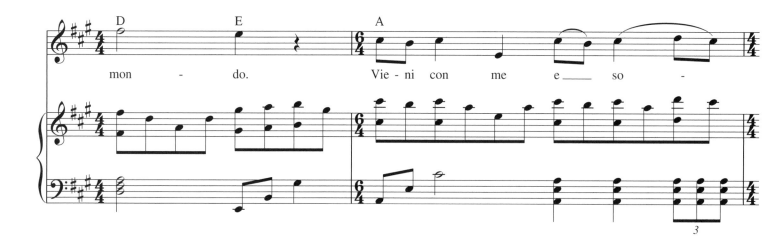

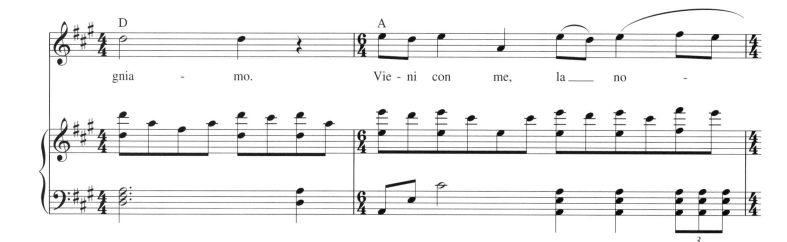

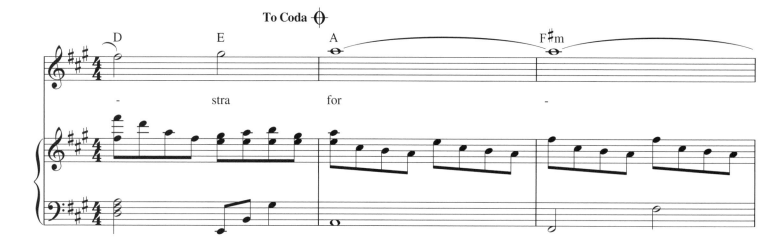

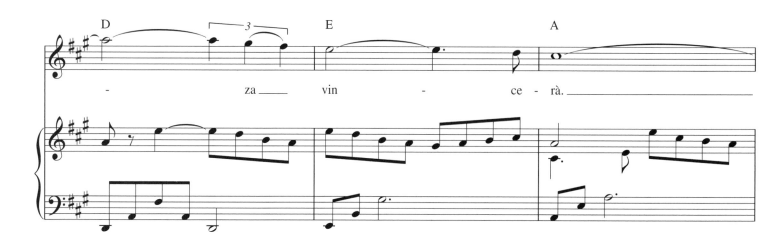

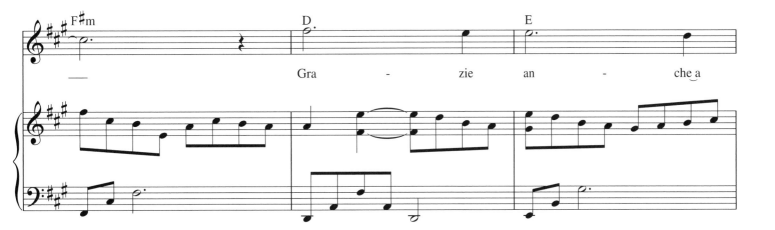

Gra - zie an - che a

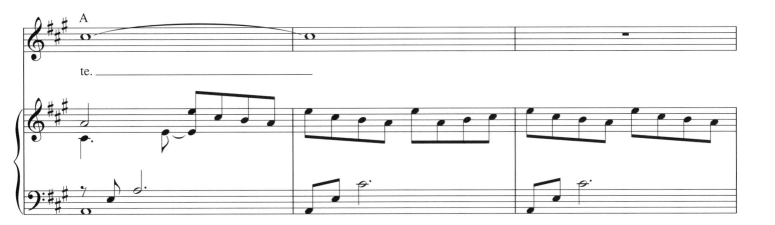

te. _____

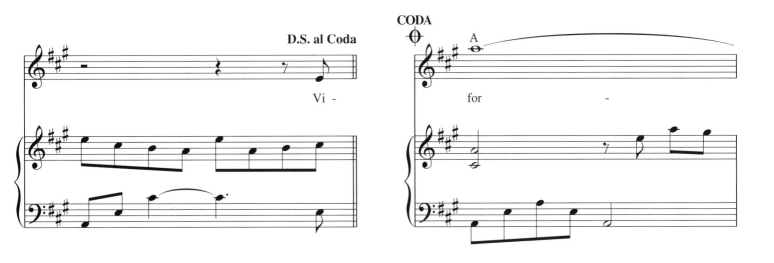

D.S. al Coda

Vi -

CODA

for -

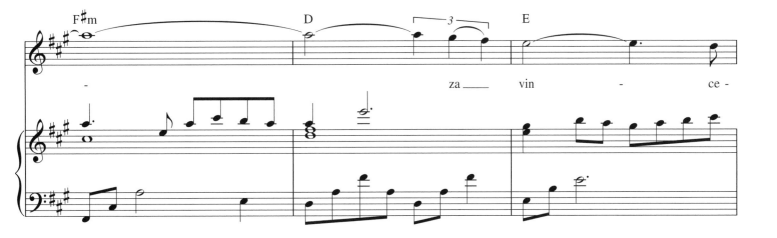

- za ___ vin - ce -

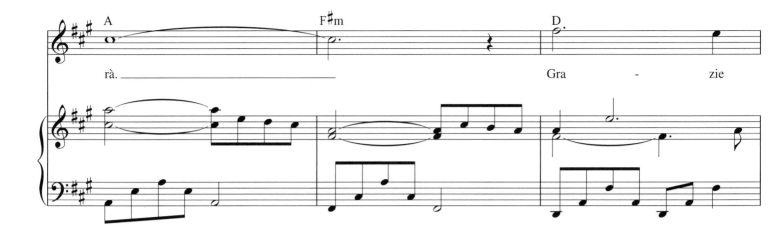

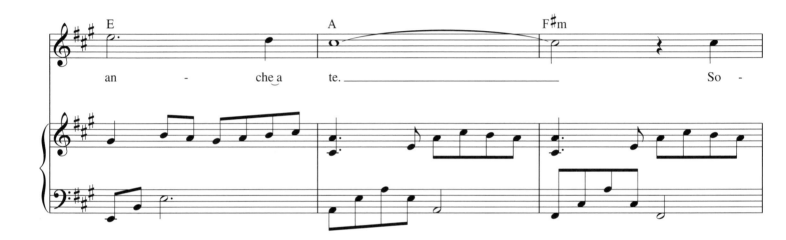

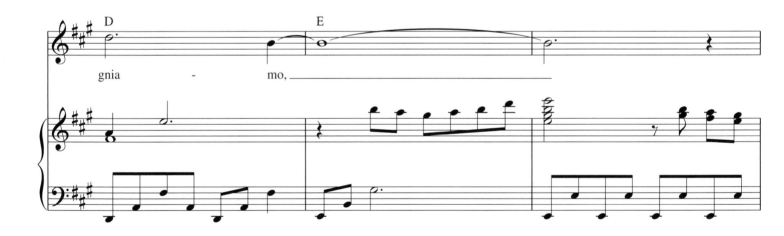

THE KEEPER

Words and Music by YANNI,
RIC WAKE, LESLIE MILLS,
ERIC SANICOLA and KEMDI

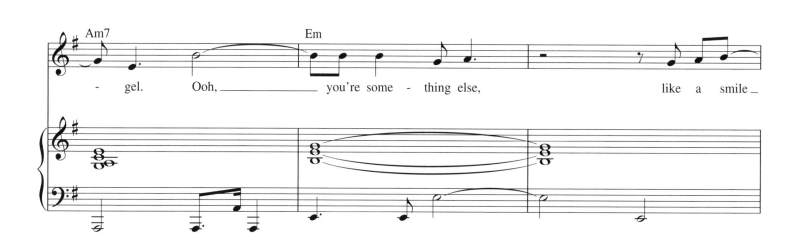

- gel. Ooh, _____ you're some - thing else, like a smile _

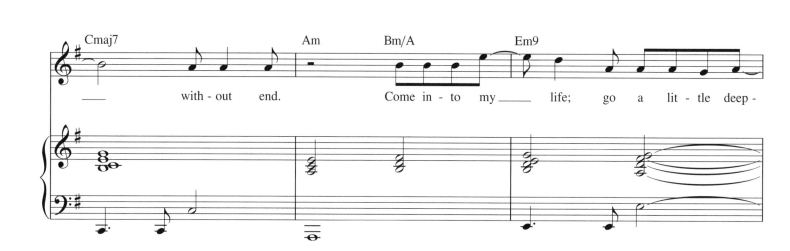

_ with - out end. Come in - to my _ life; go a lit - tle deep -

- er. Come in - to my _ life; you could be the keep - er.

You're pull - ing me clos - er _ and you're

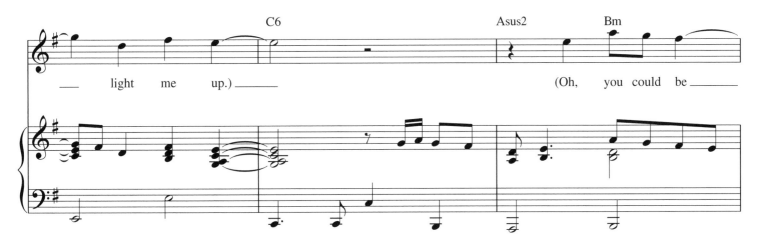

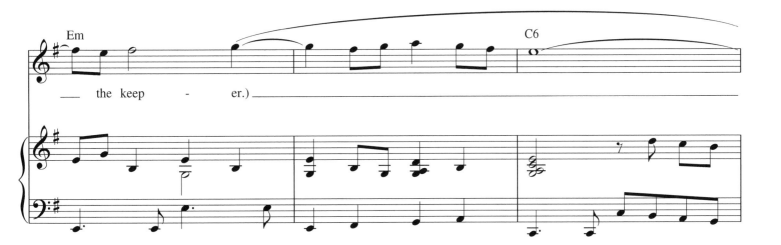

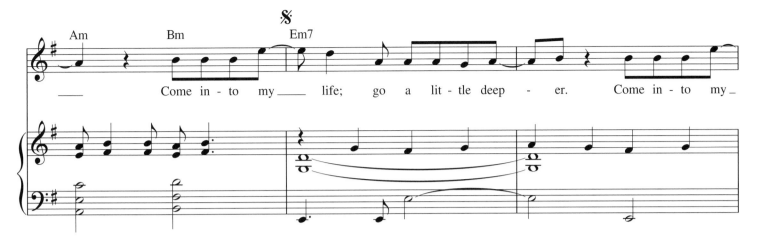

Come in-to my ___ life; go a lit-tle deep - er. Come in-to my ___

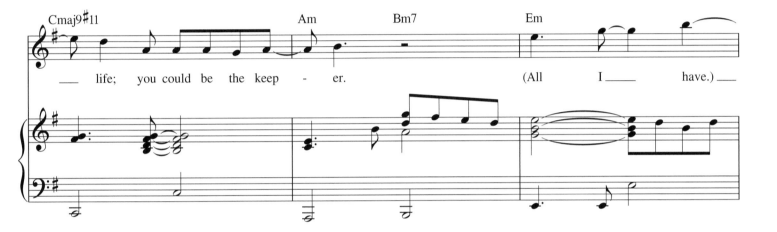

___ life; you could be the keep - er. (All I ___ have.) ___

You're pull-ing me clos - er ___ and you're flow - ing in. ___

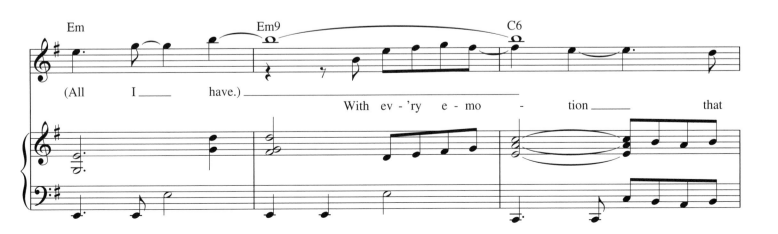

(All I ___ have.) ___ With ev-'ry e - mo - tion ___ that

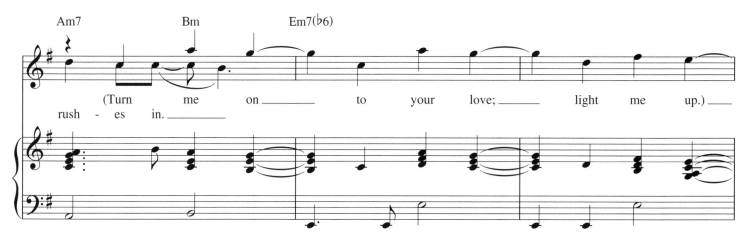

(Turn me on ____ to your love; ____ light me up.) ____
rush - es in. ____

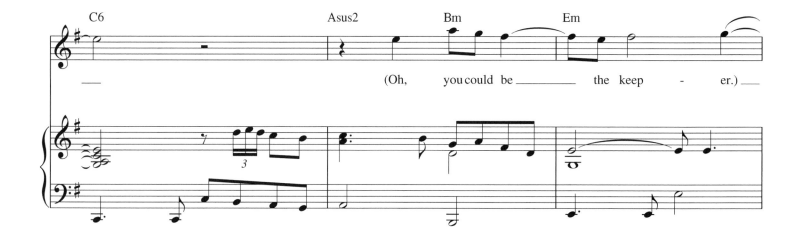

____
(Oh, you could be ____ the keep - er.) ____

To Coda ⊕

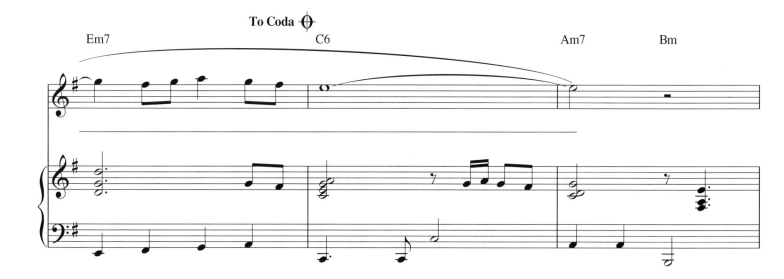

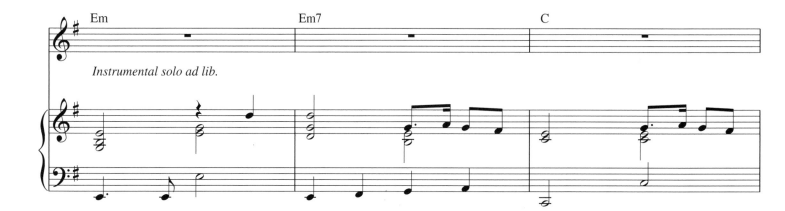

Instrumental solo ad lib.

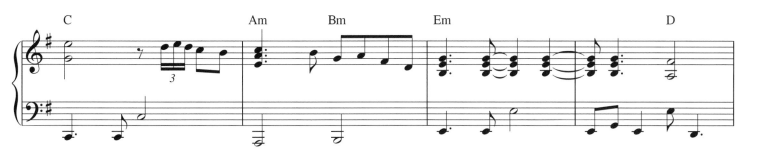

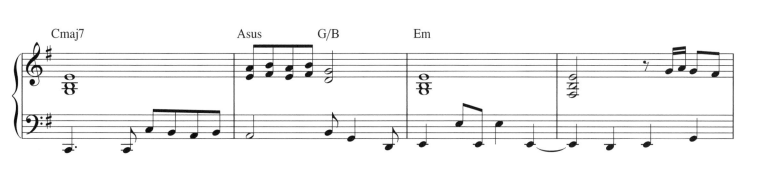

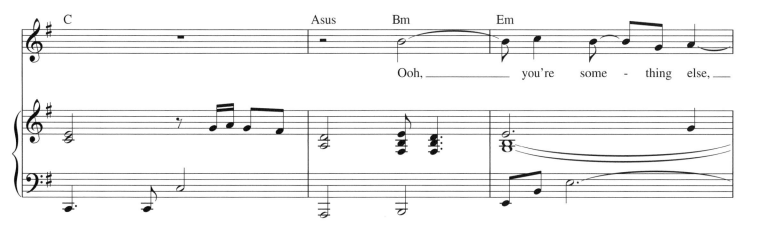

Ooh, _____ you're some - thing else, __

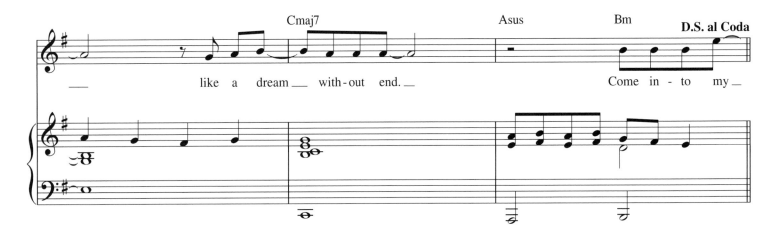

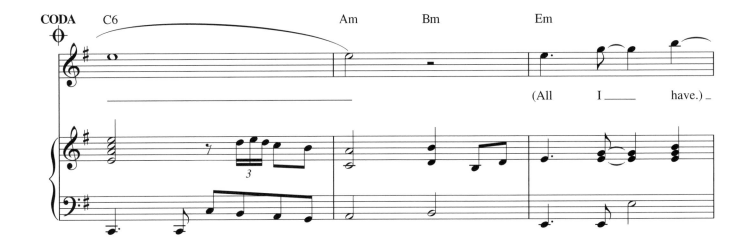

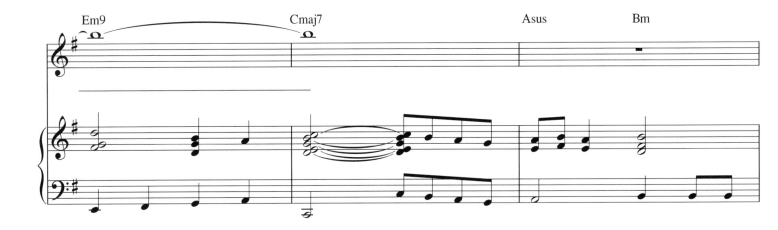

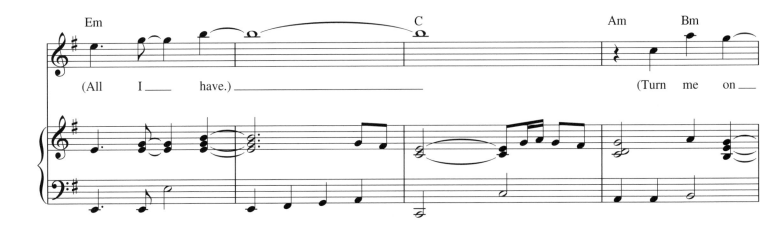

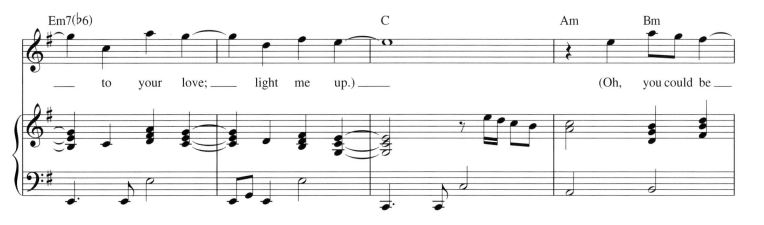

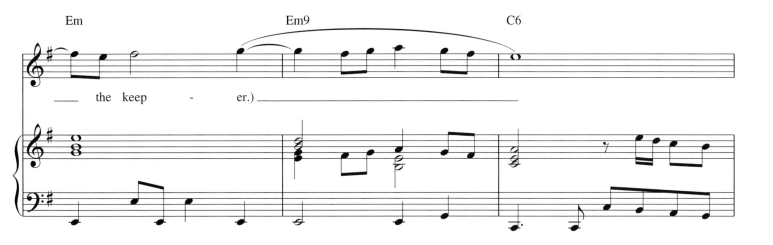

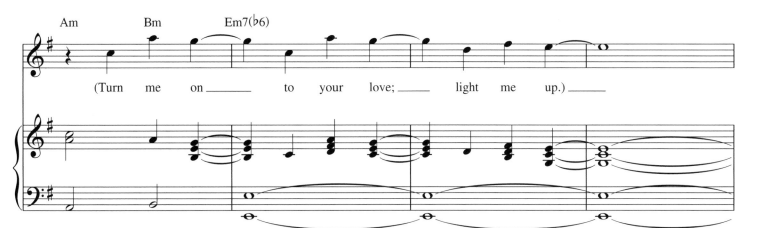

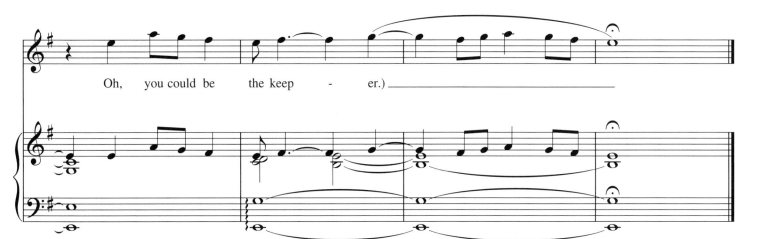

OUR DAYS

Words and Music by YANNI,
MIKLOS MALEK, LESLIE MILLS
and CHRIS PELCER

Moderately

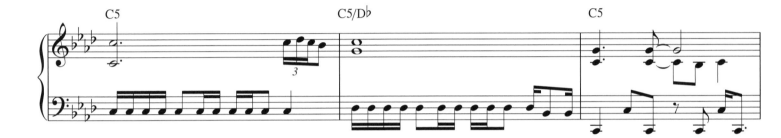

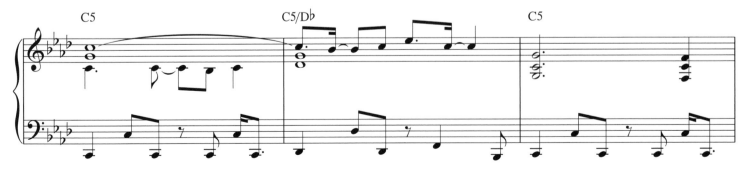

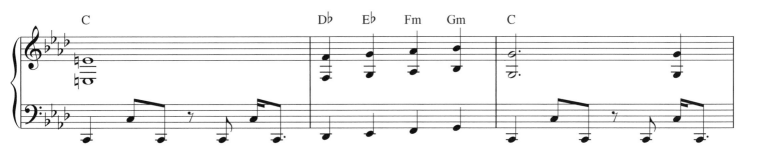

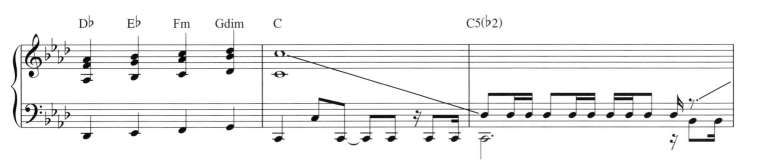

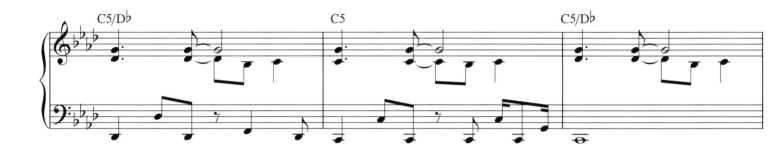

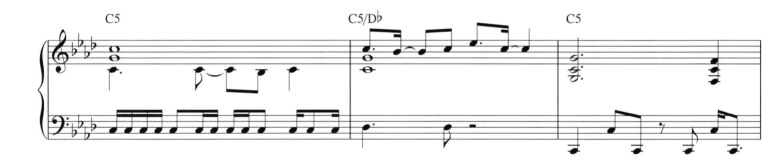

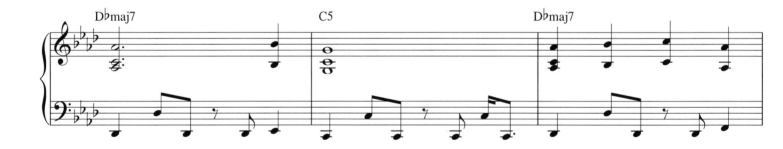

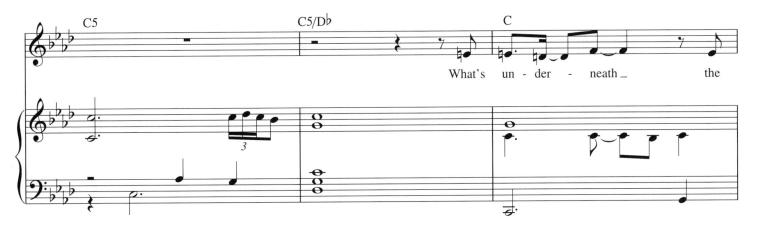

What's un - der - neath __ the warm - est __ wa - ter? What's in your __ dreams __ that's

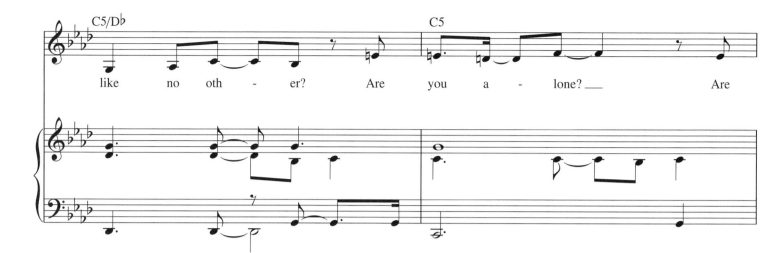

like no oth - er? Are you a - lone? ___ Are

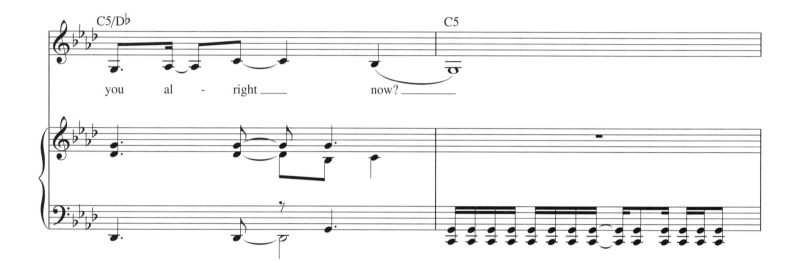

you al - right ___ now? ___ Are

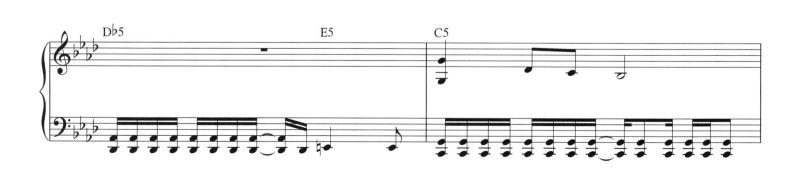

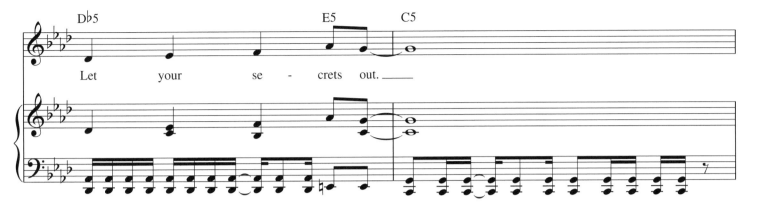

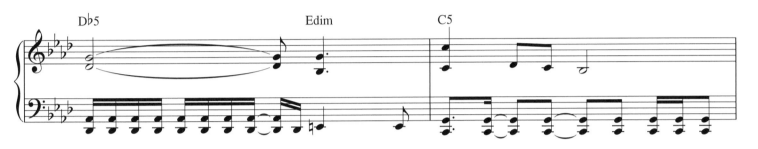

Let your se - crets out. _____

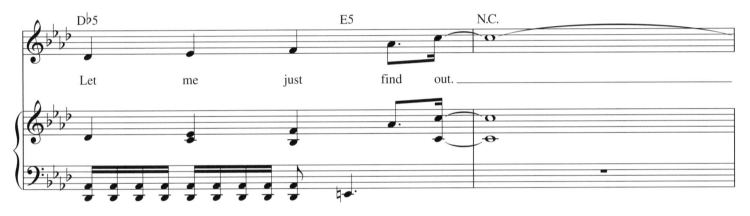

Let me just find out. _____

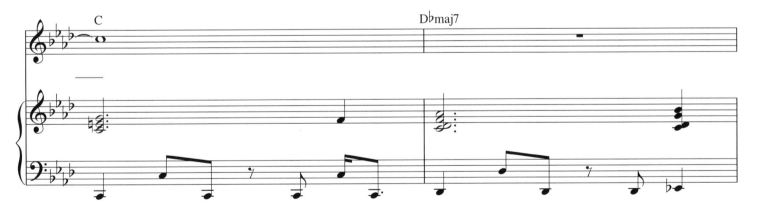

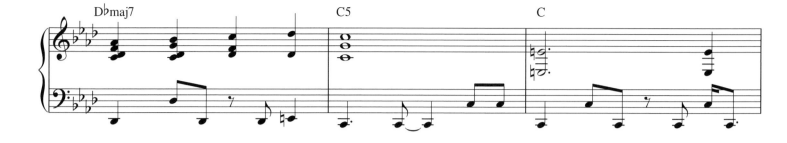

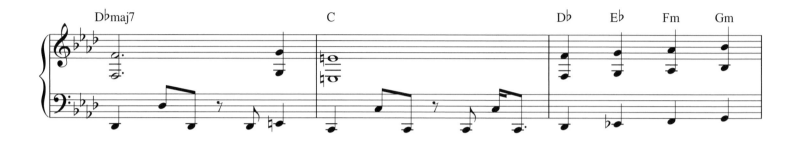

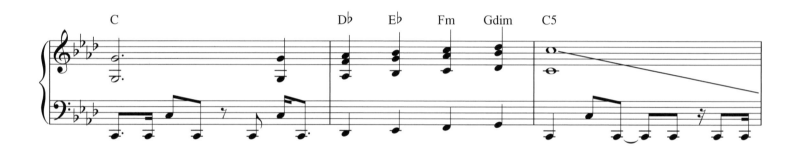

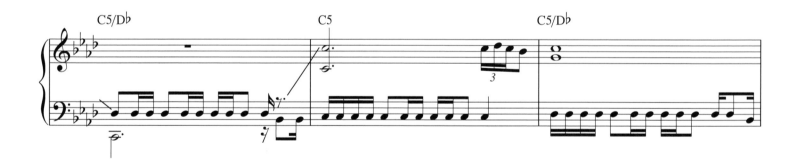

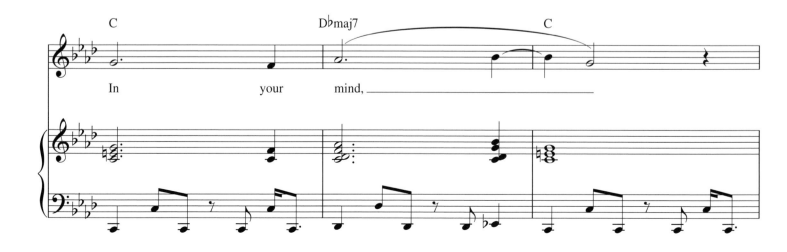

In your mind, _____

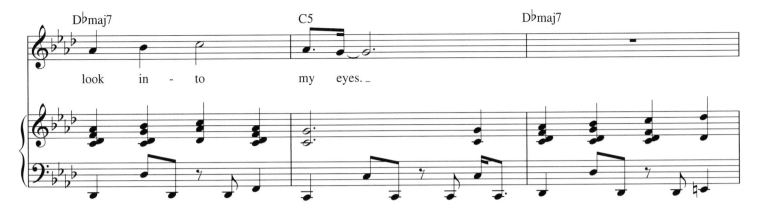

look in - to my eyes. _

In your

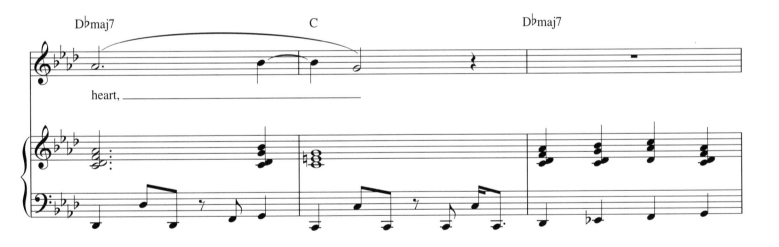

heart, ___

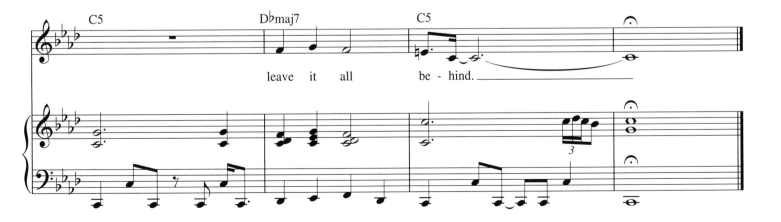

leave it all be - hind. ___

NEVER LEAVE THE SUN

Words and Music by LESLIE MILLS
and CHRIS PELCER

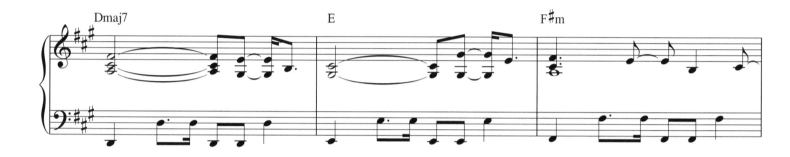

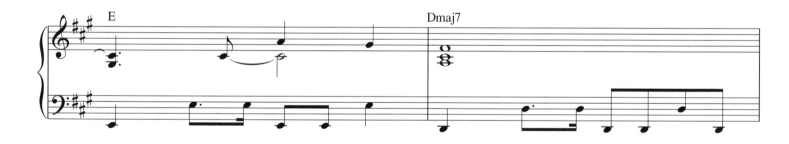

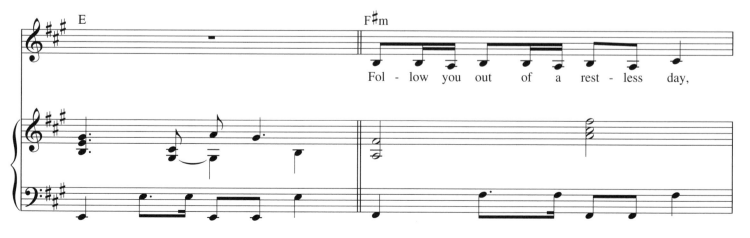

Fol- low you out of a rest- less day,

walk - ing a road where the dream can change. _

_ You caught me there _ where my mind was lost, _____

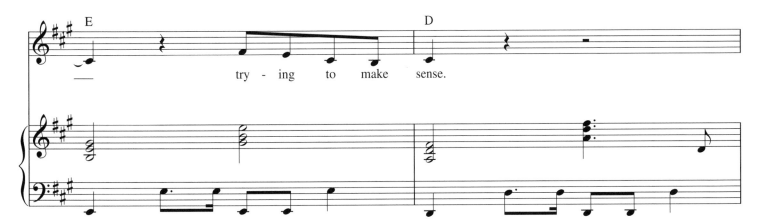

_ try - ing to make sense.

Show me the world with an o - pen heart, _____

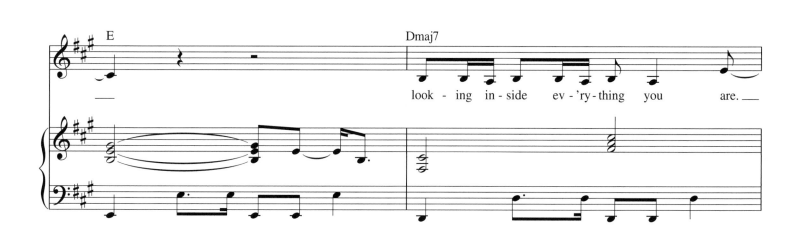

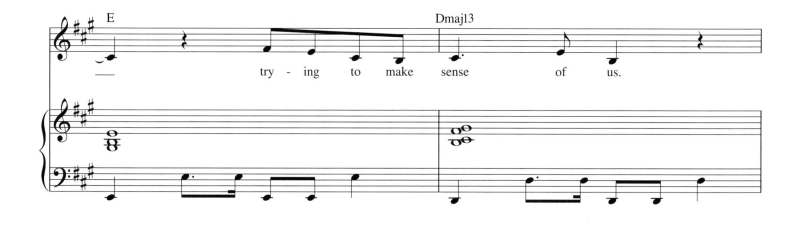

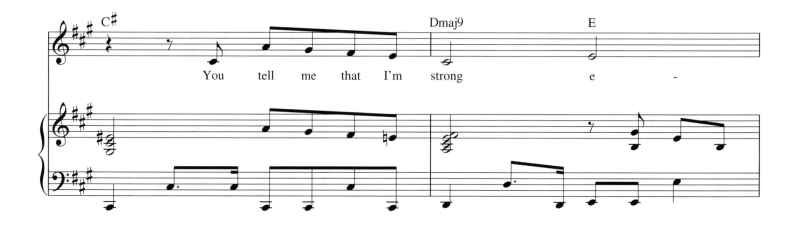

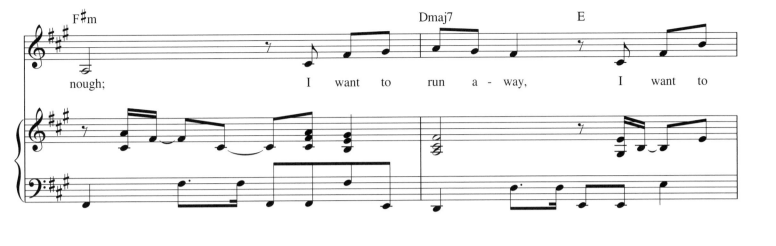

nough; I want to run a - way, I want to

fly in - to your arms and nev - er leave the

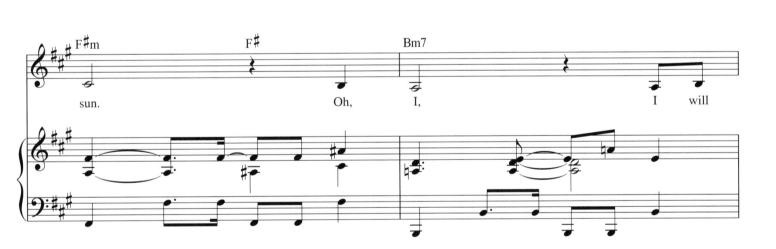

sun. Oh, I, I will

nev - er leave the sun. _____

(Oh, no, no, no, no, no, no.) _____

(Oh, no, no, no, no, no, no.)

Some-where be-tween want-ing to be-lieve

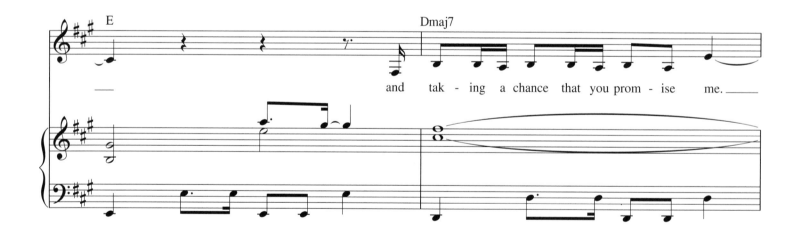

and tak-ing a chance that you prom-ise me.

Some-where be-tween ev-'ry morn and dawn,

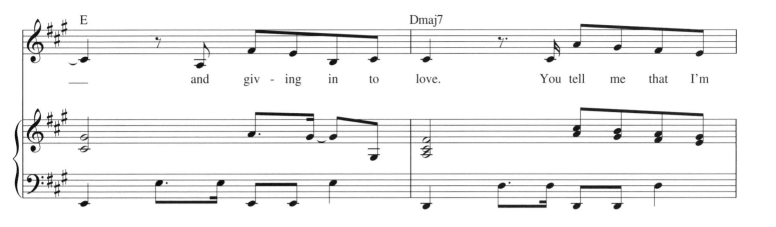

and giv - ing in to love. You tell me that I'm

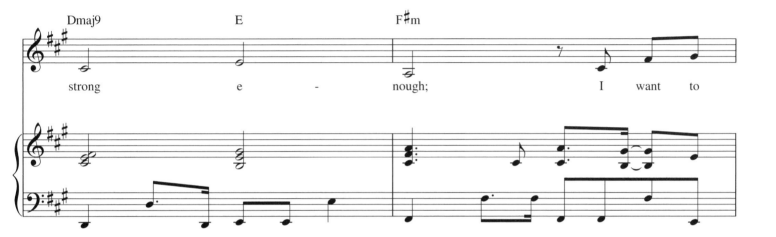

strong e - nough; I want to

run a - way, I want to fly in - to your arms and nev - er

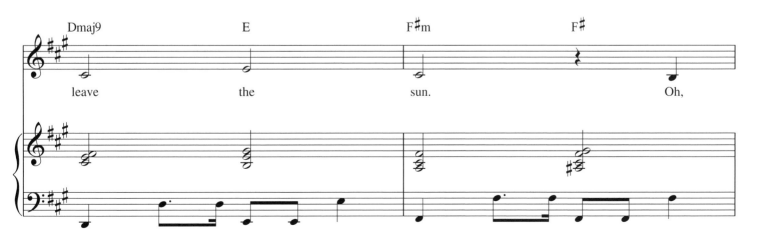

leave the sun. Oh,

I, I will nev - er leave the sun. _

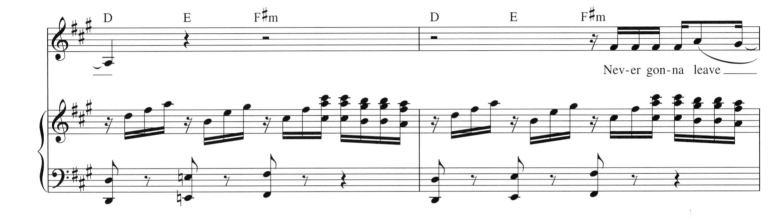

Nev-er gon-na leave _

_ the sun. _

Tell me, ___ you tell me that I'm strong _ e-nough; I'm nev -

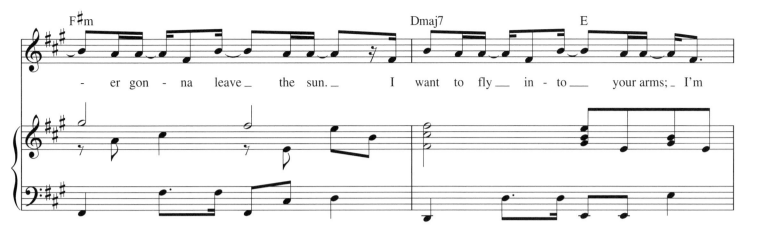

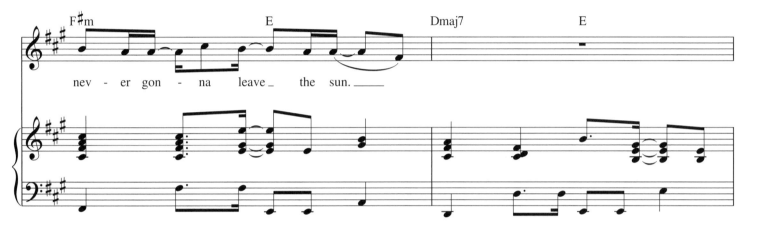

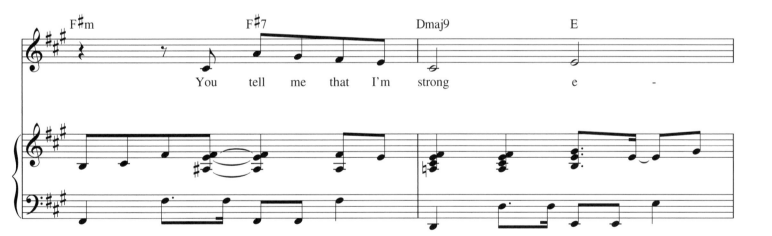

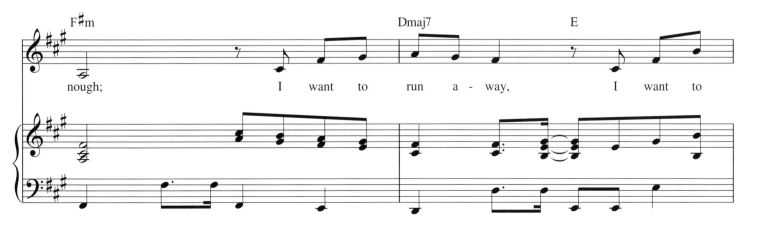

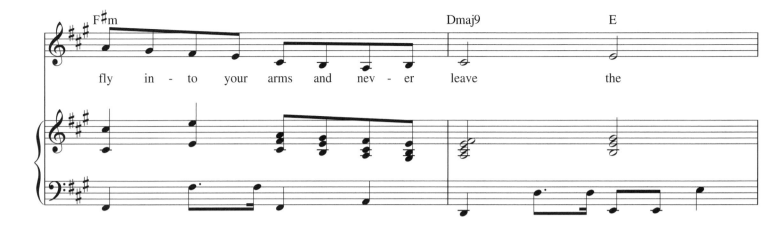

fly in - to your arms and nev - er leave the

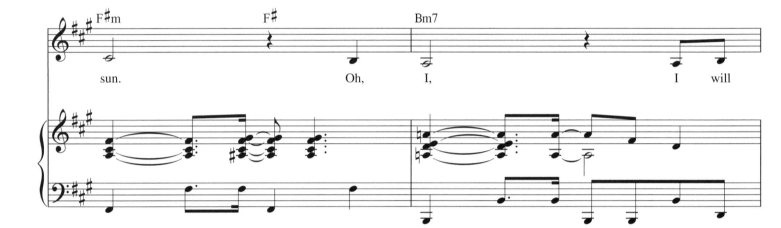

sun. Oh, I, I will

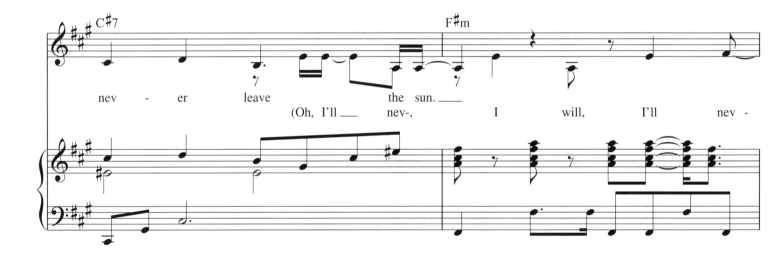

nev - er leave (Oh, I'll ___ nev-, the sun. ___ I will, I'll nev -

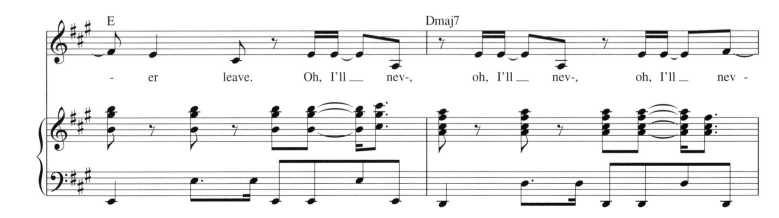

- er leave. Oh, I'll ___ nev-, oh, I'll ___ nev-, oh, I'll ___ nev -

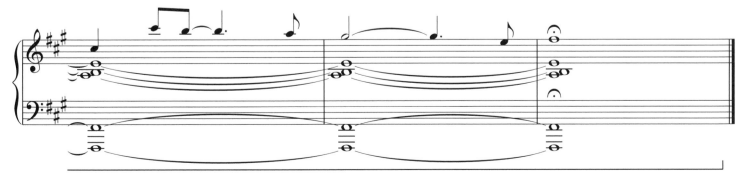

BEFORE THE NIGHT ENDS

Music by YANNI
Lyrics by LESLIE MILLS

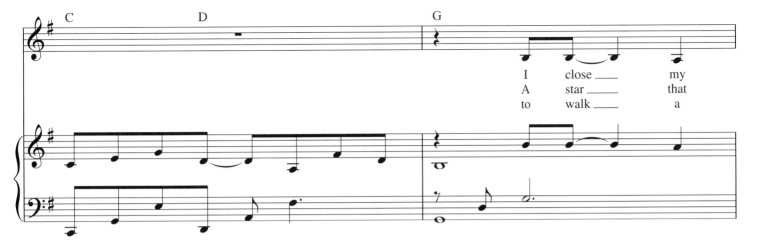

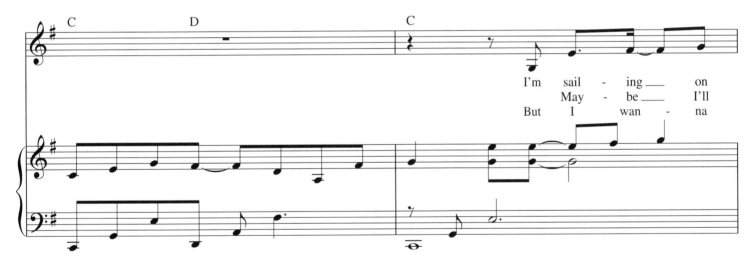

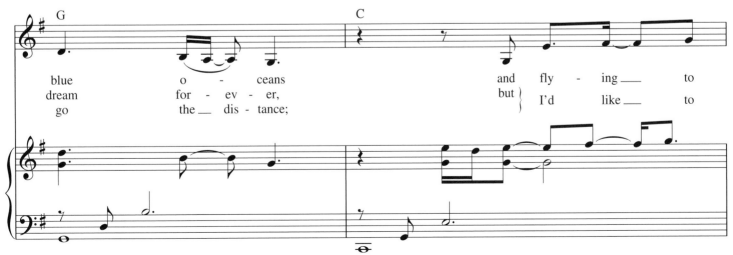

40

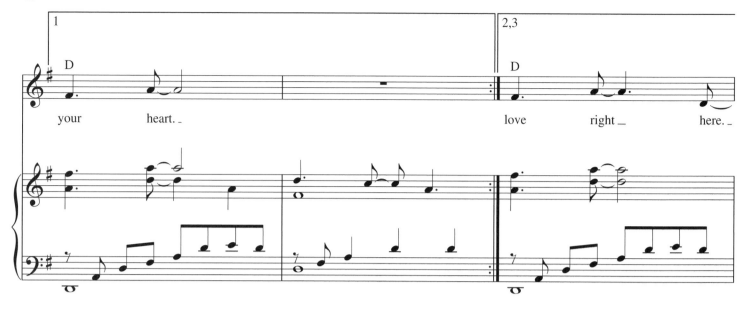

your heart. love right here.

Be - fore the night ends

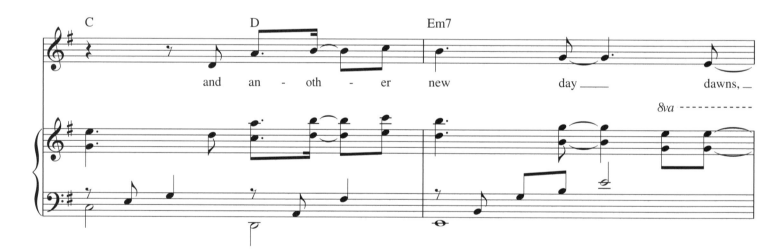

and an - oth - er new day dawns,

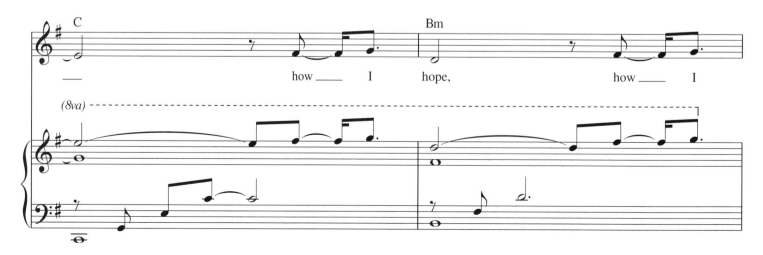

how I hope, how I

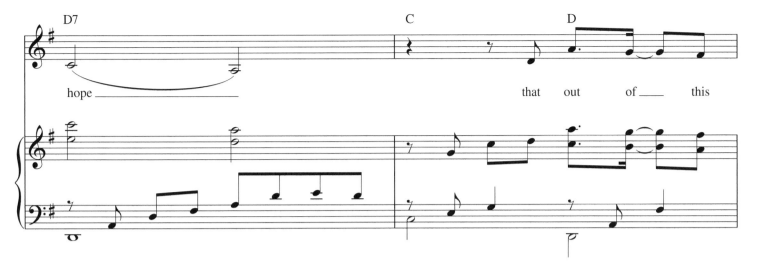

hope _____ that out of _____ this

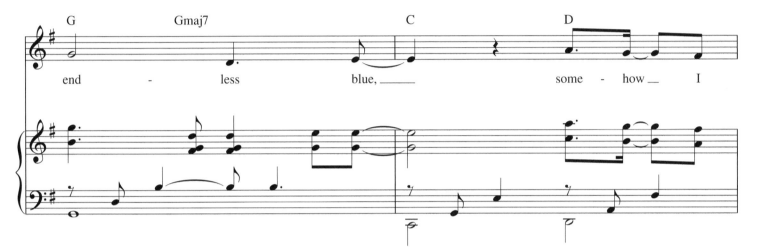

end - less blue, _____ some - how _ I

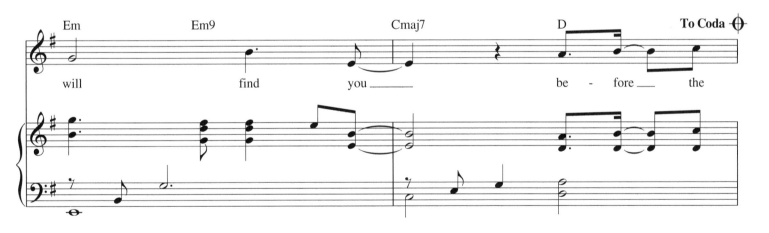

will find you _____ be - fore _ the

To Coda

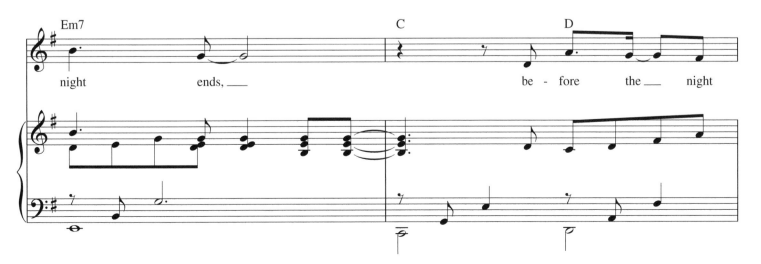

night ends, _____ be - fore the _ night

42

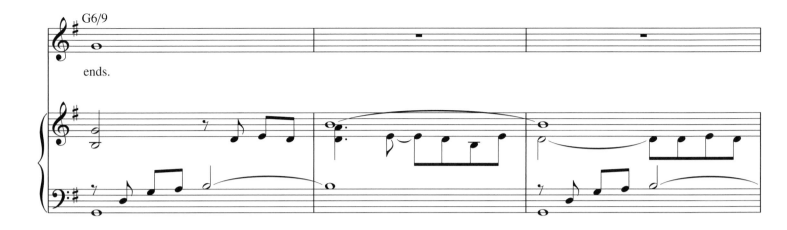

D.S. al Coda
(take 3rd ending)

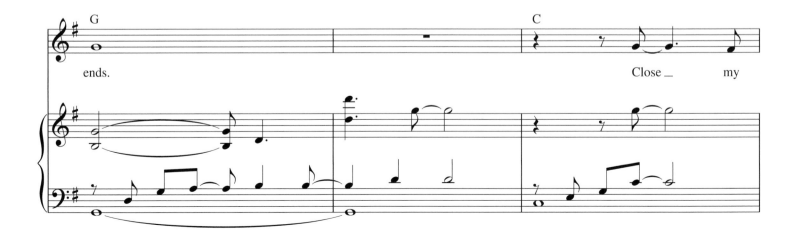

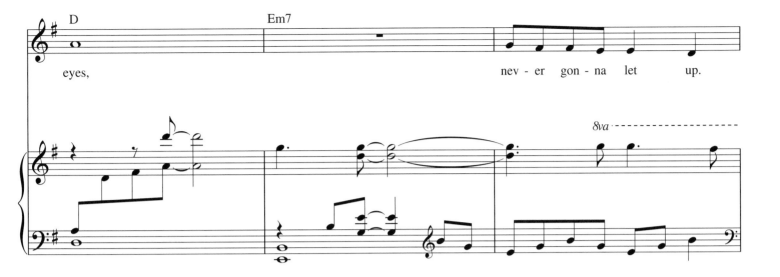

eyes,   nev - er gon - na let   up.

Be - fore _ the night _____

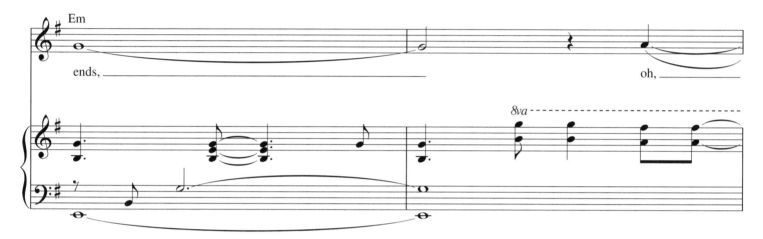

ends, _____ oh, _____

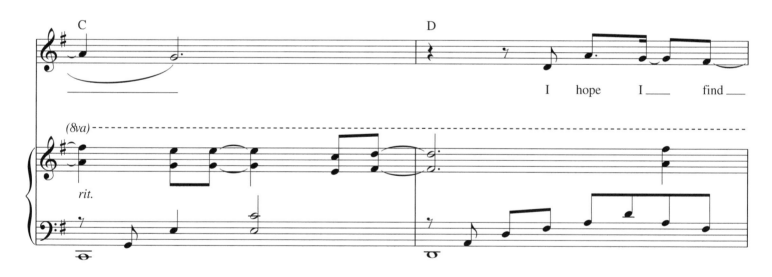

I hope I ___ find ___

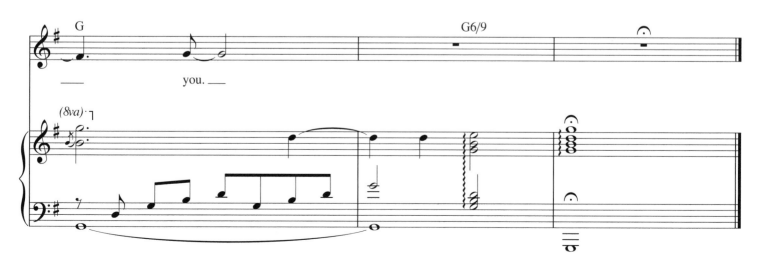

___ you. ___

1001

Words and Music by YANNI
and MIKLOS MALEK

Moderately slow

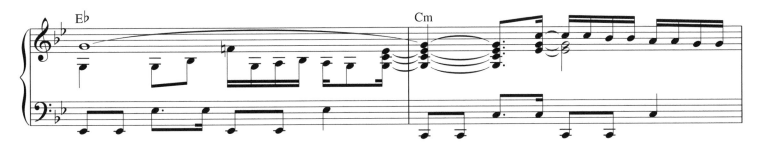

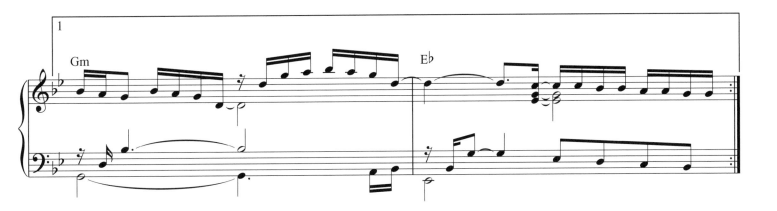

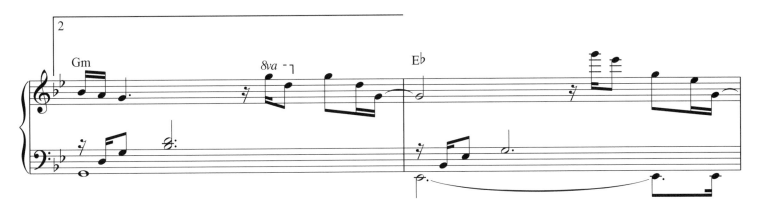

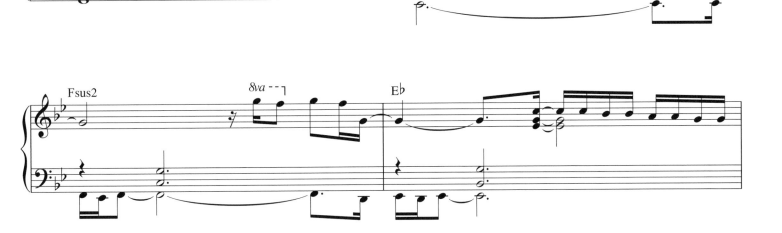

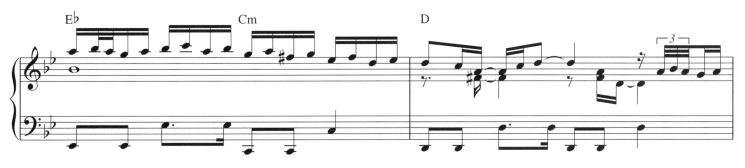

MAS ALLÁ

Words and Music by YANNI,
ENDER THOMAS and FERNANDO OSORIO

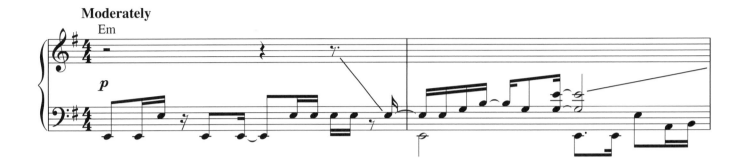

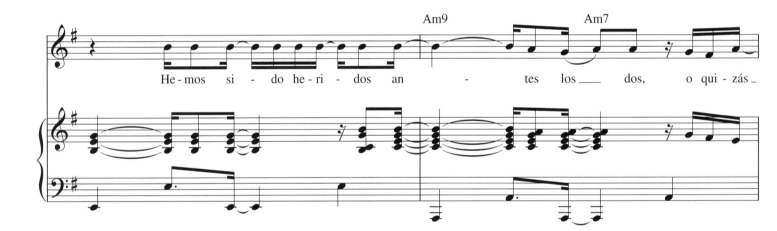

He-mos si-do he-ri-dos an - tes los ___ dos, o qui-zás ___

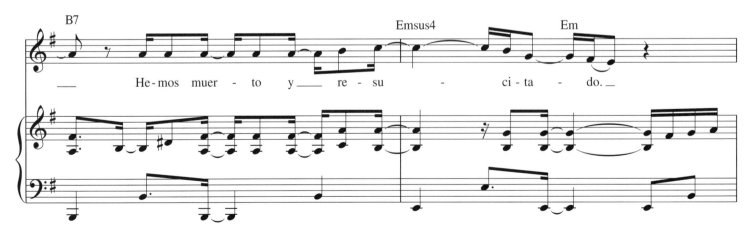

___ He-mos muer - to y ___ re-su - ci-ta - do. ___

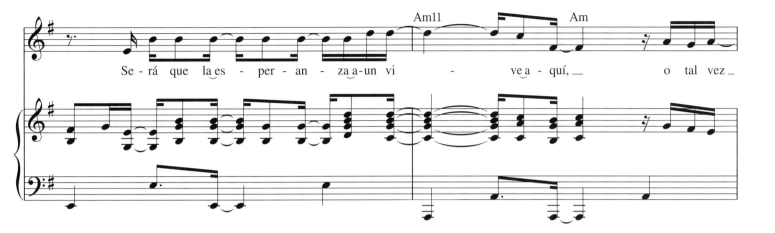

Será que la es - pe - ran - za a-un vi - ve a-quí, __ o tal vez __

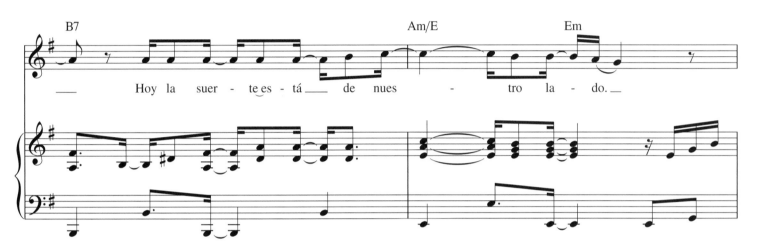

Hoy la suer - te es - tá __ de nues - tro la - do. __

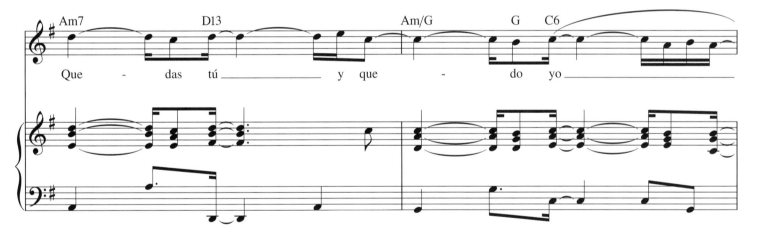

Que - das tú __ y que - do yo __

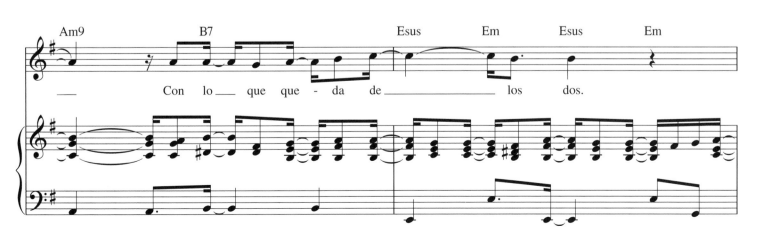

Con lo __ que que - da de __ los dos.

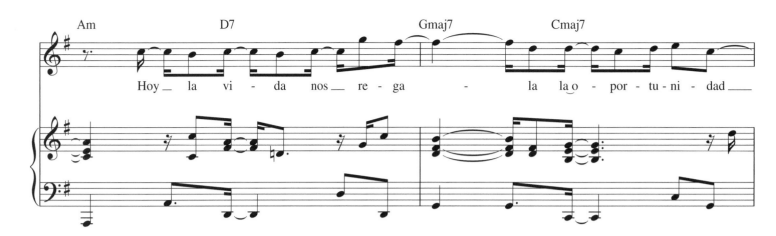

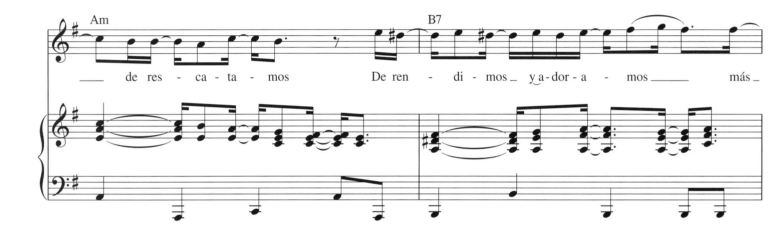

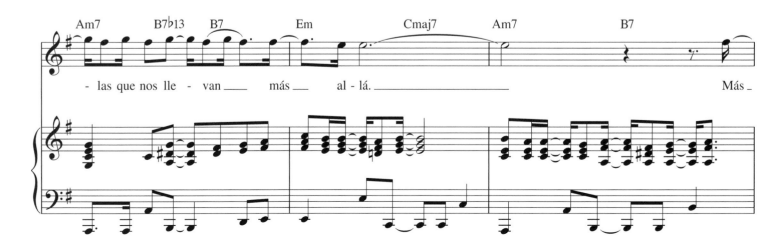

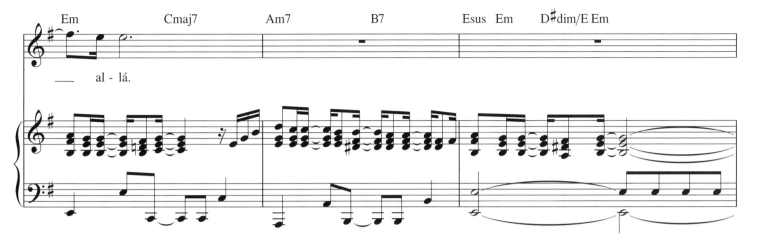

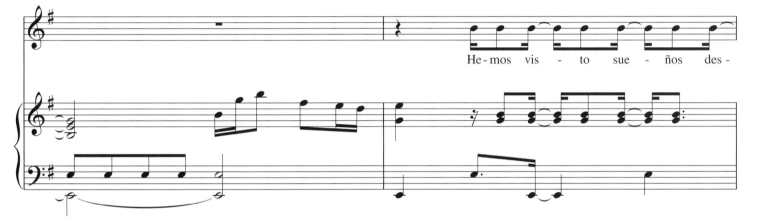

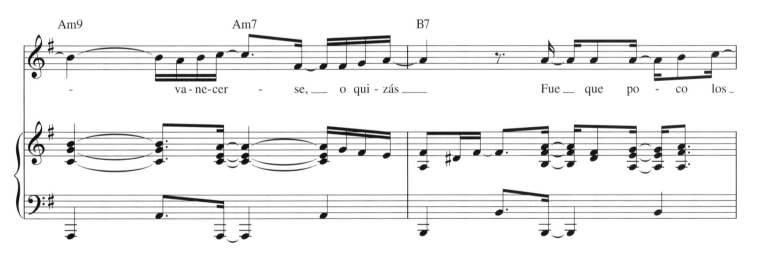

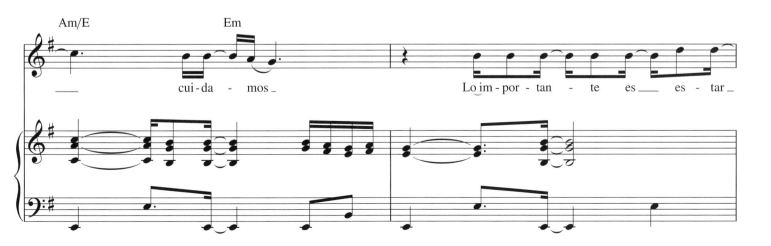

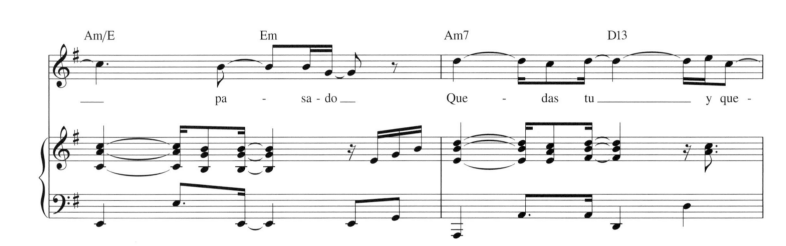

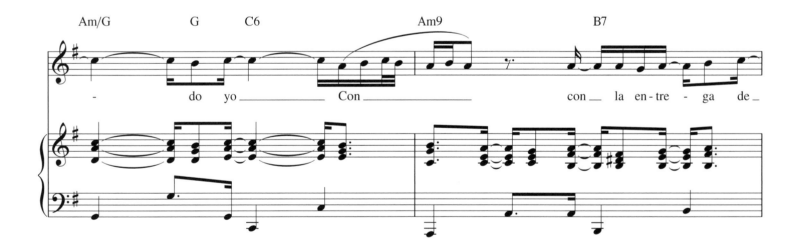

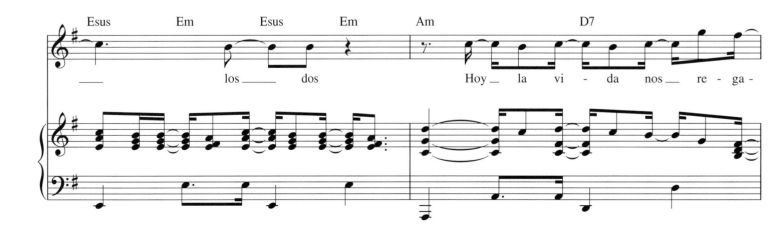

Más ___ al - lá _____
Más _____ al - lá. ___

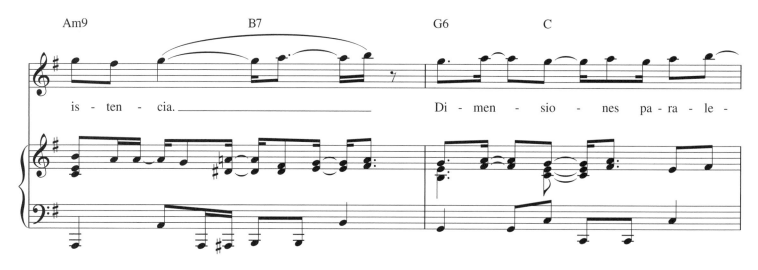

___ de la con - cien - cia   más ___ al - lá.   Más al - lá de la ex-

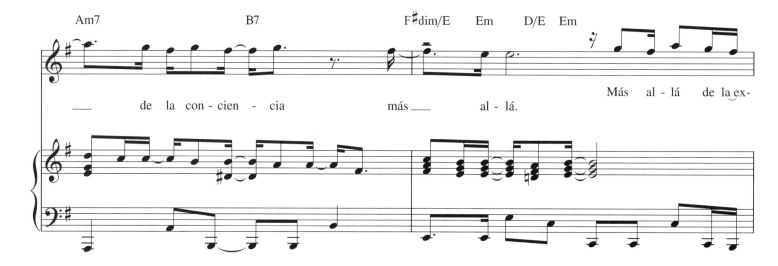

is - ten - cia. _____   Di - men - sio - nes pa - ra - le -

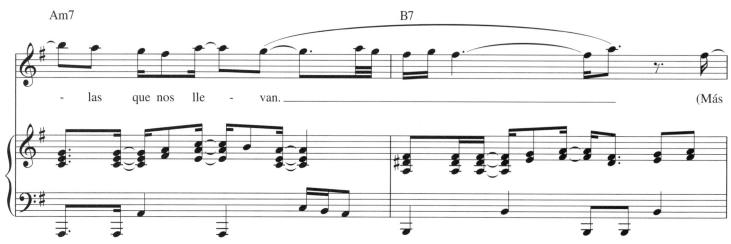

- las que nos lle - van. _____   (Más

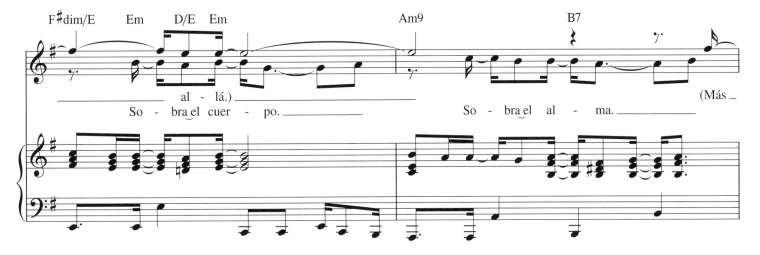

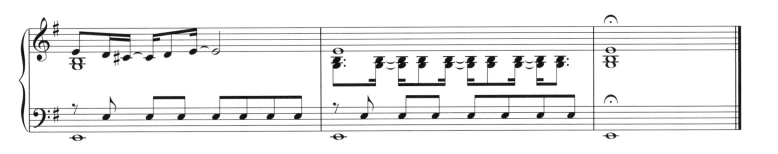

UNICO AMORE

Music by YANNI
Lyrics by NATHAN PACHECO

Animated

La lu-ce del - le stel - le scin-til-la ___ sul
oc - chi ___ bril - lan - ti, pro - fon-di co - me il

ma - re il lu-mi-na ___ il mi - o a - mo -
ma - re in - can-ta-no ___ co - me si - re -

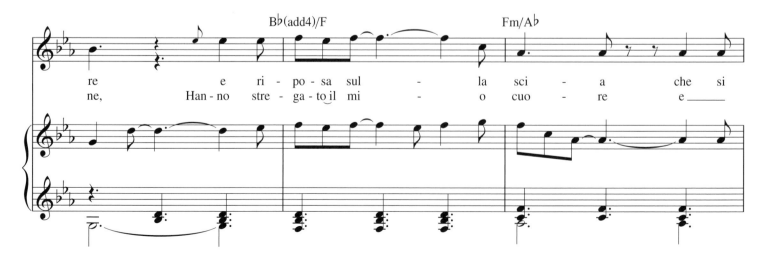

re e ri-po-sa sul - la sci - a che si
ne, Han - no stre-ga-to il mi - o cuo - re e ___

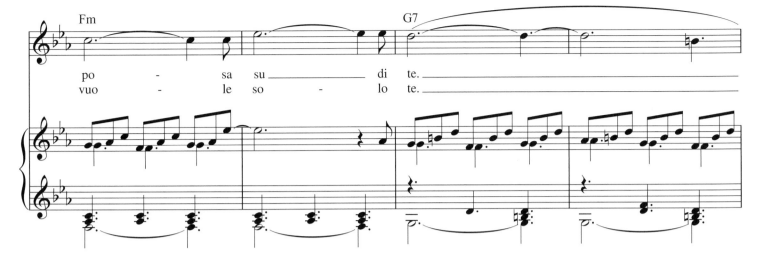

pri - gio - nie - ro del - la tu a bel -

lez - za, mi per - do af - fo -

gan - do tra le tue brac - cia

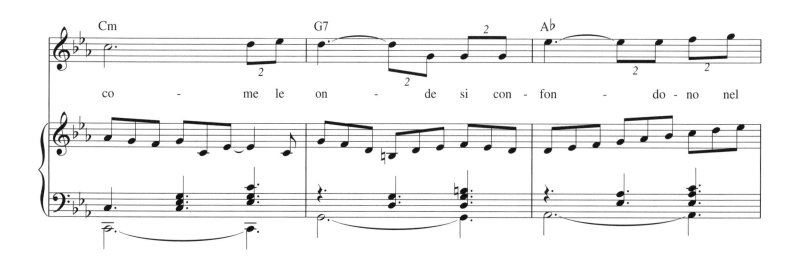

co - me le on - de si con - fon - do - no nel

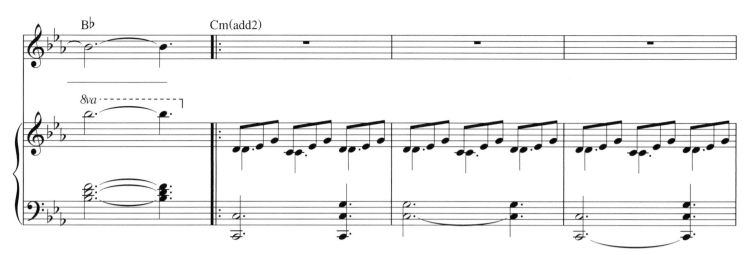

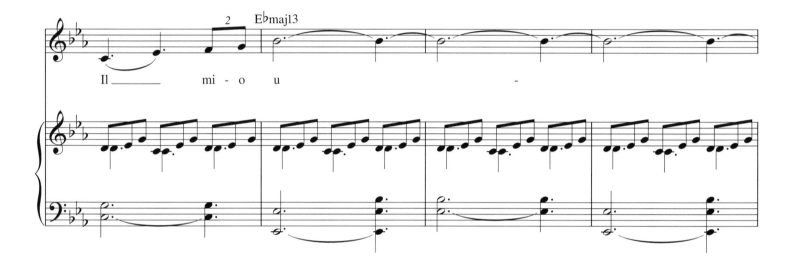

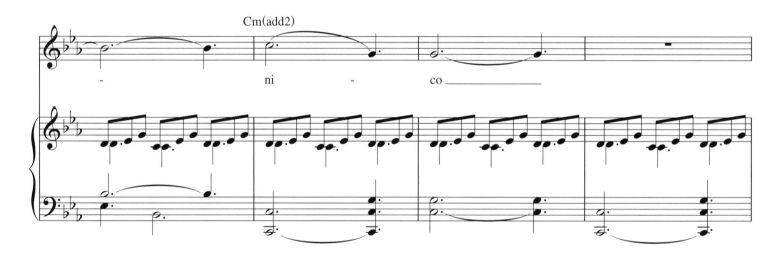

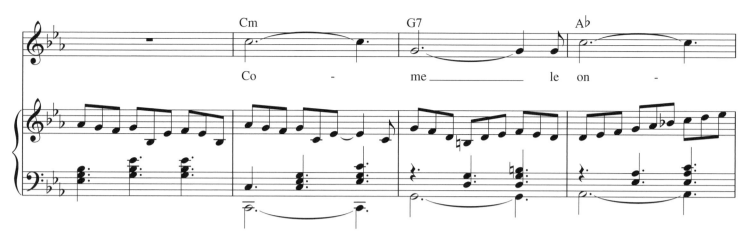

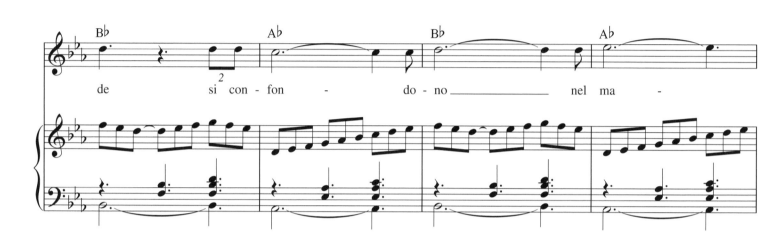

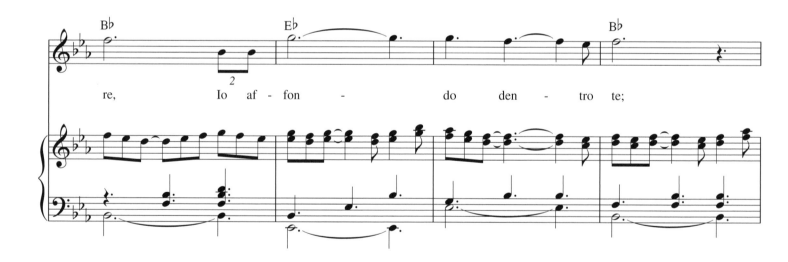

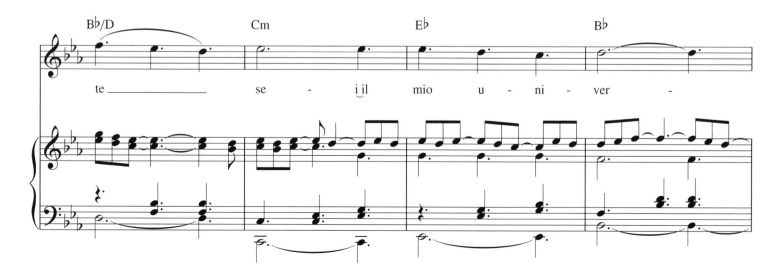

so. Io af - fon - do _____ den - tro te,

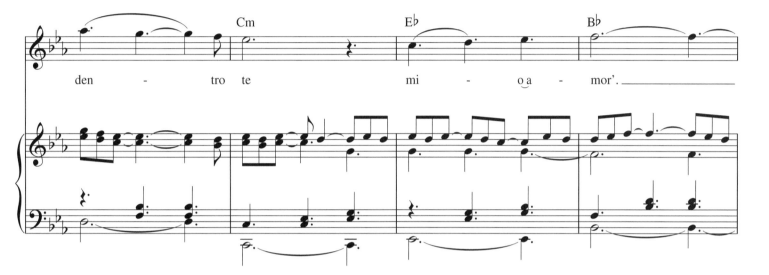

den - tro te mi - o a - mor'. _____

Freely

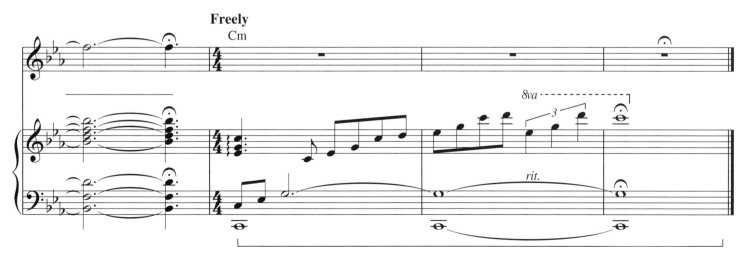

VIVI IL TUO SOGNO

Music by YANNI
Lyrics by NATHAN PACHECO

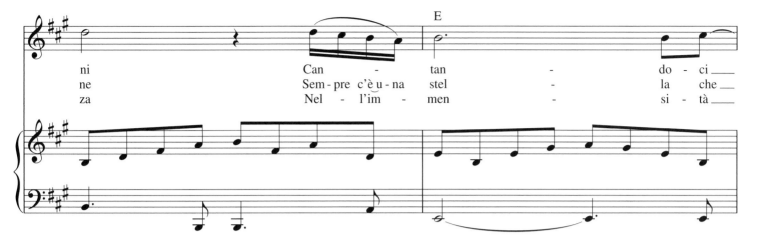

ni - ci
Can - tan - do ci___
ne
Sem - pre c'è u - na stel - la che___
za
Nel - l'im - men - si - tà___

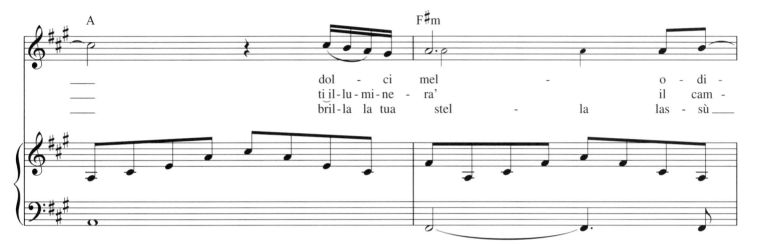

___ - ci mel - o - di -
ti il - lu - mi - ne - ra'
il cam -
___ bril - la la tua stel - la las - sù___

- e
A - scol - ti - a - mo il mi -
mi - no'
(2., 3.) E___ li da - van - ti a

ste - ro del cie - lo.
te la puoi ve -
Cer -

68

de - re. Si, con __ l'a - mo -

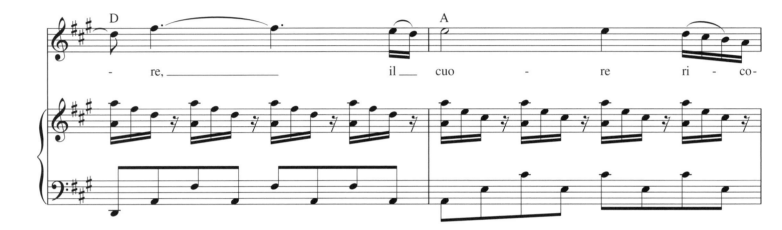

- re, __ il __ cuo - re ri co-

min - cia a so - gnare. __ Las - cia - lo vo - la -

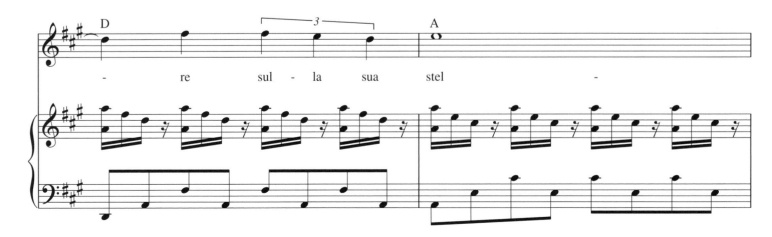

- re sul - la sua stel -

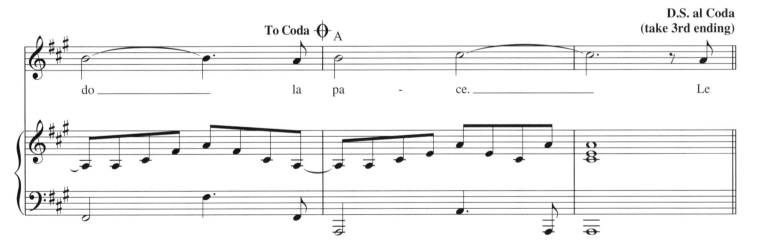

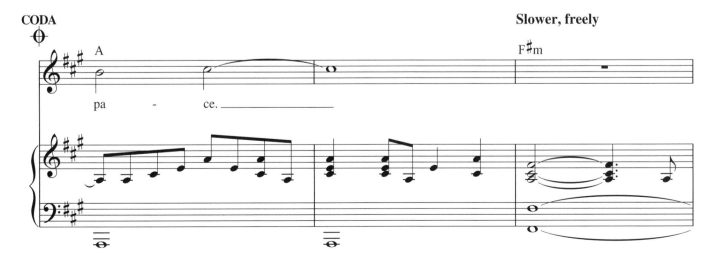

"So - gna! So -

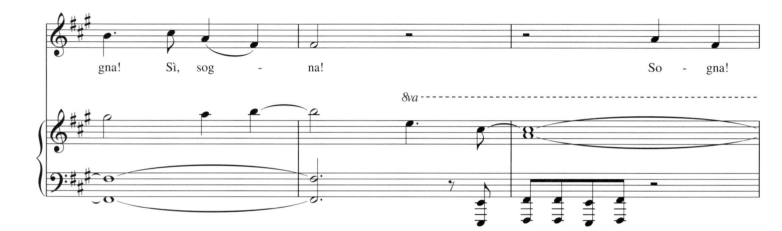

gna! Sì, sog - na! So - gna!

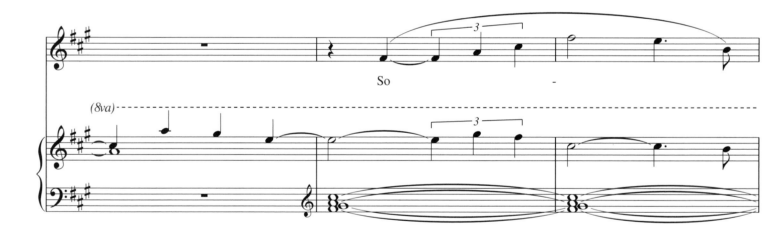

So -

gna! Sì, so - gna!"

ORCHID

Words and Music by YANNI
and ERIC SANICOLA

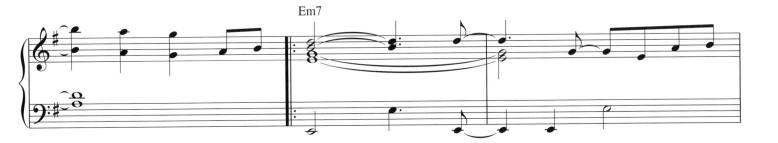

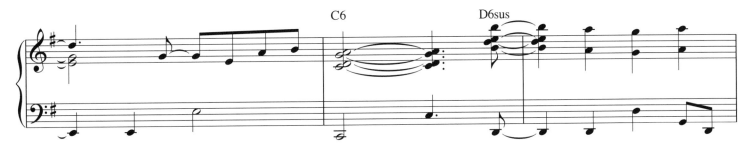

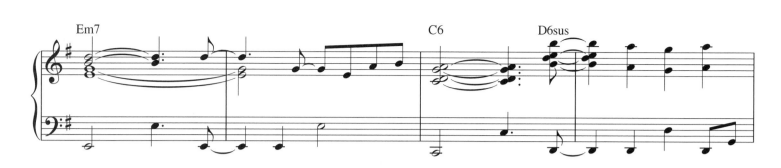

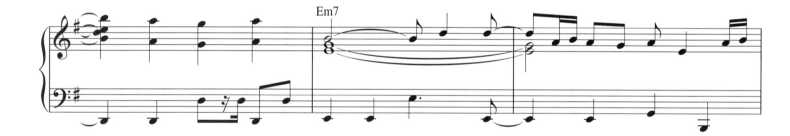

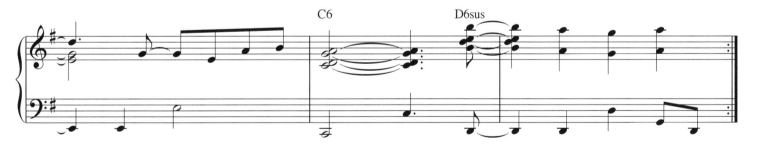

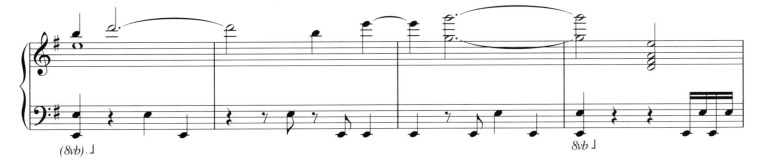

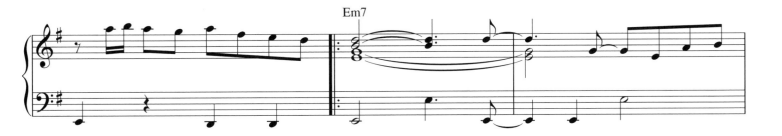

SET ME FREE

Words and Music by YANNI,
MARC RUSSELL, DAVID SCHEUER
and CHLOE LOWERY

Moderately slow

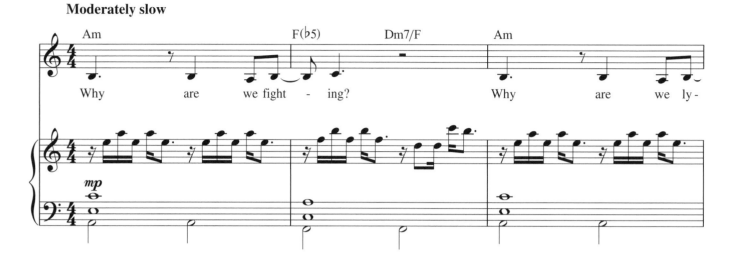

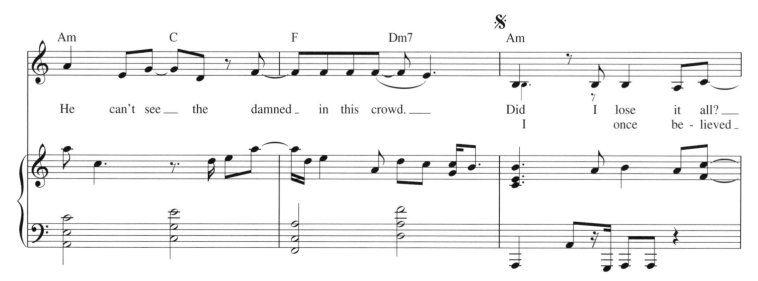

How did I miss the call?
hon - es - ty was key, _____ but

Con - form me _____ to an im - age of a doll, ___
I can't stay _____ and live _____ this way _____ 'cause

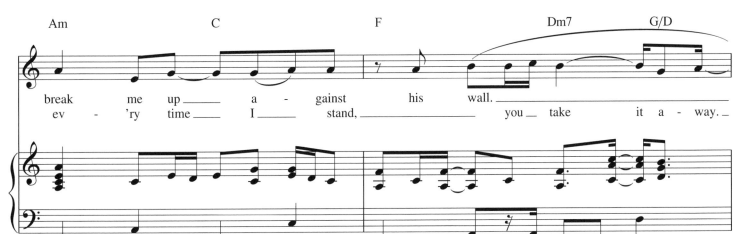

break me up _____ a - gainst his wall. _____
ev - 'ry time _____ I _____ stand, _____ you take it a - way. ___

___ I can't look in the mir - ror and see my-self stand - ing there; ___

all I see ___ is an il - lu - sion, fight - ing a ___

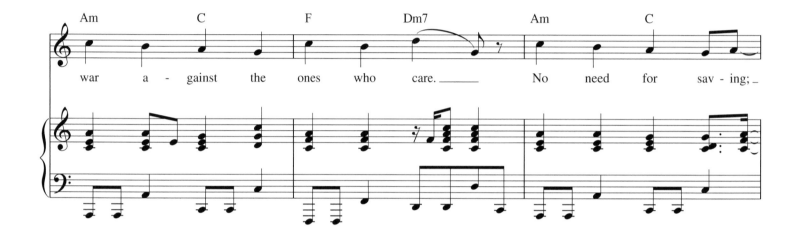

war a - gainst the ones who care. ___ No need for sav - ing; ___

To Coda ⊕

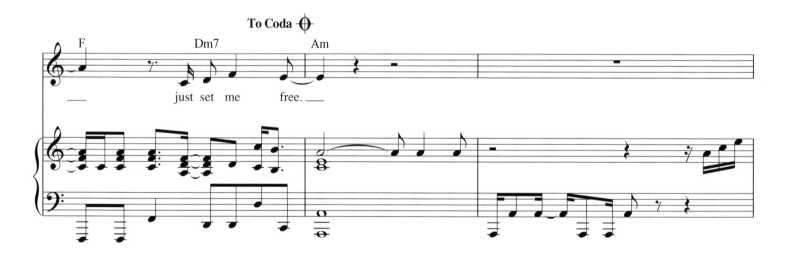

just set me free. ___

Can you please for - give ___ me? Words can't say the mak-

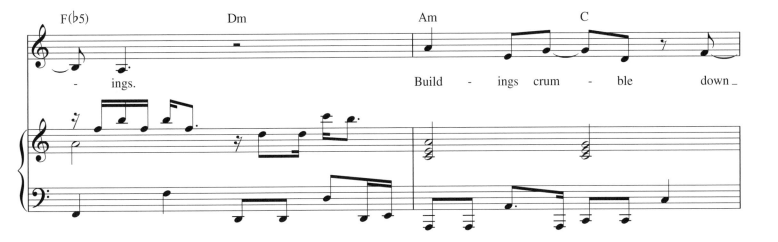

-ings. Build - ings crum - ble down _

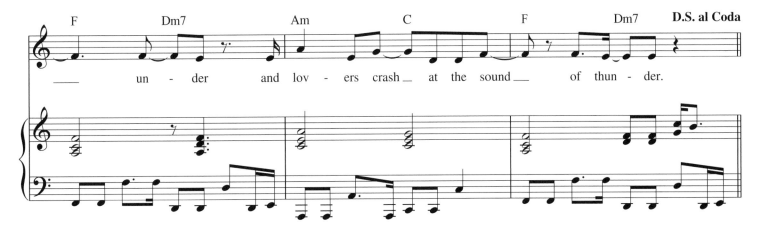

D.S. al Coda

_ un - der and lov - ers crash _ at the sound _ of thun - der.

CODA

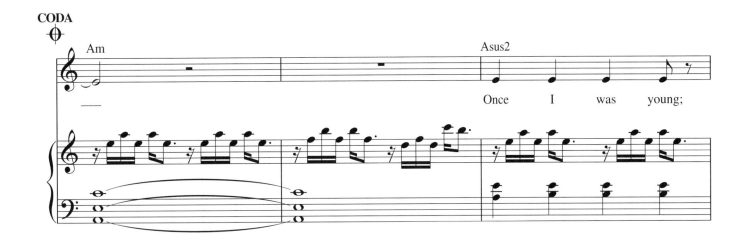

Once I was young;

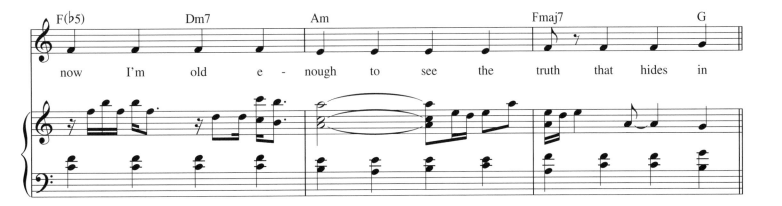

now I'm old e - nough to see the truth that hides in

me. } I can't look __ in the mir - ror and see my-self stand - ing there. __

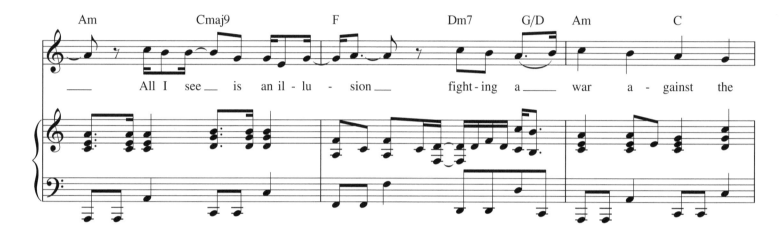

__ All I see __ is an il - lu - sion __ fight - ing a __ war a - gainst the

ones who care. ____ No need for sav - ing; ____ just set me __ free.

No need for sav - ing; ____ just set me free. ____

KILL ME WITH YOUR LOVE

Words and Music by YANNI,
MARC RUSSELL, DAVID SCHEUER
and CHLOE LOWERY

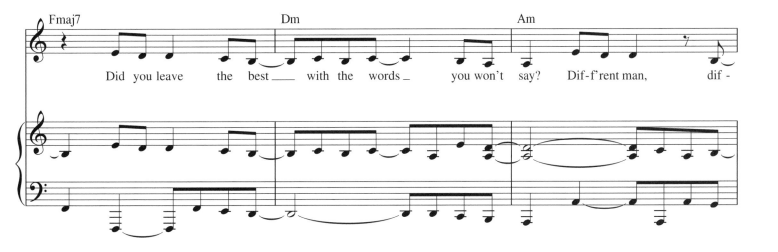

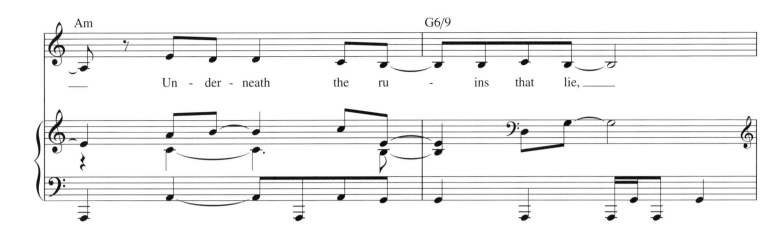

Un - der - neath the ru - ins that lie, _____

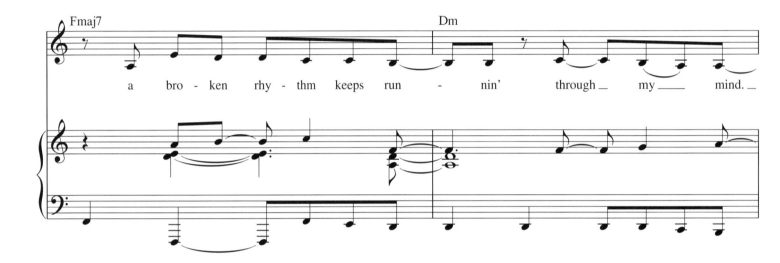

a bro - ken rhy - thm keeps run - nin' through _ my _ mind.

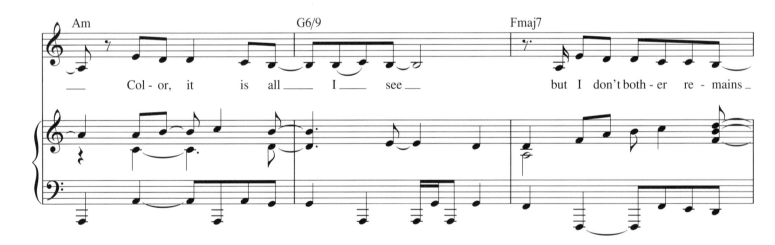

_ Col - or, it is all _ I _ see _ but I don't both - er re - mains _

_ of you _ and _ me. And I trust you to kill _ me with _ your love. _

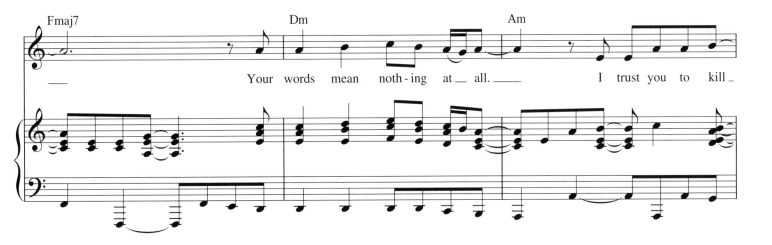

Your words mean noth-ing at __ all. __ I trust you to kill __

__ me with __ your love; __ your words mean noth-ing at __ all.

Ah. _____

My ob-ses-sion lies __ in this room; __

va - cant mem - o - ries haunt ___ me through ___ and ___ through. ___

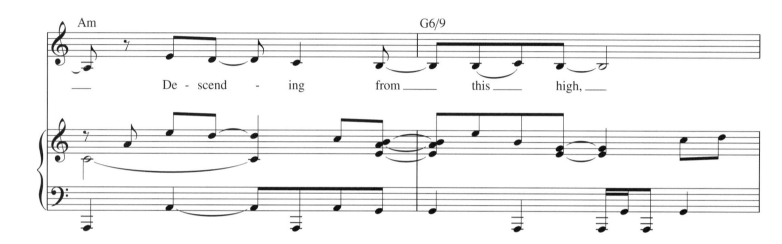

___ De - scend - ing from ___ this ___ high, ___

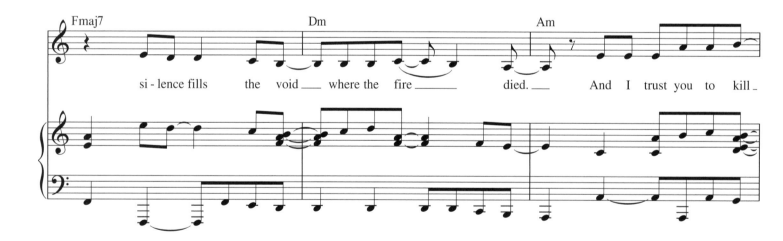

si - lence fills the void ___ where the fire ___ died. ___ And I trust you to kill ___

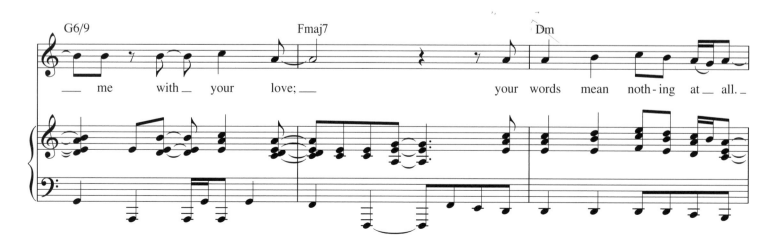

___ me with ___ your love; ___ your words mean noth - ing at ___ all. ___

I trust you to kill ___ me with ___ your love; ___ your

words mean noth-ing at ___ all. _____ Ah, _____

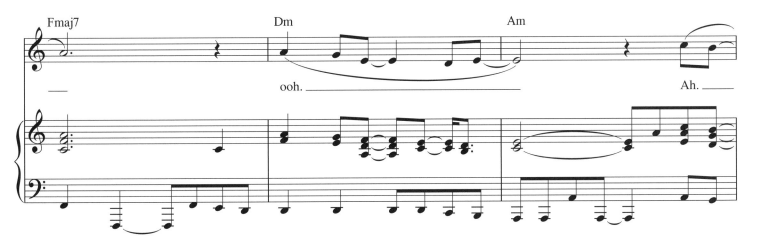

___ ooh. _____ Ah. ____

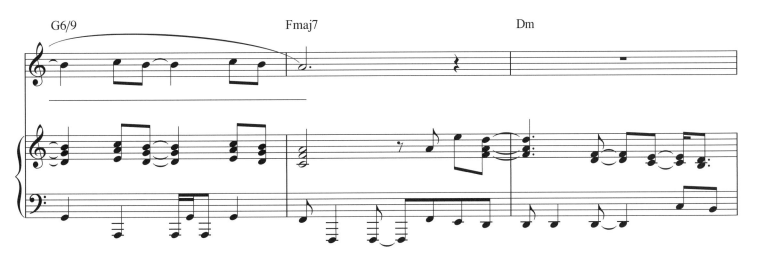

And I trust you to kill __

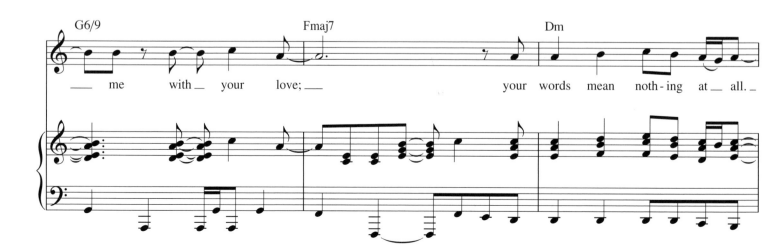

__ me with __ your love; __ your words mean noth-ing at __ all. __

I trust you to kill ___ me with ___ your love; ___ your

words mean noth-ing at ___ all. ___ Ah, ___

___ your words mean noth-ing at ___ all. ___ Ah, ___

your words mean noth-ing at ___ all. ___

And I trust you to kill ___ me with ___ your love; ___

___ your words mean noth - ing at ___ all. ___

___ I trust you to kill ___ me with ___ your love; ___

___ your words mean noth - ing at ___ all. ___

MI TODO ERES TÚ

Music by YANNI
Lyrics by CHLOE LOWERY and KARLA APONTE
Additional Music by CESAR LEMOS

Slowly, very expressively

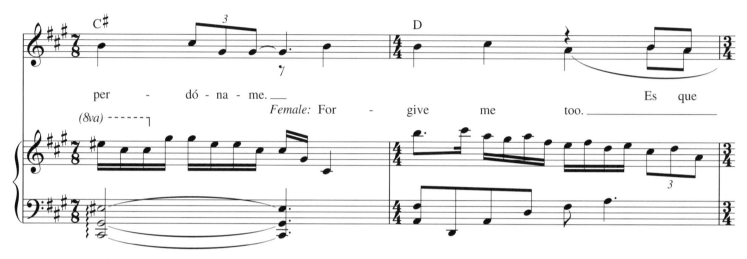

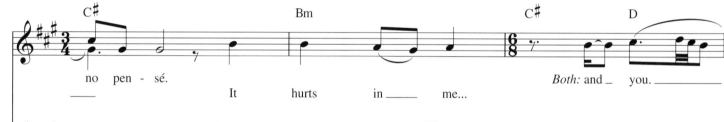

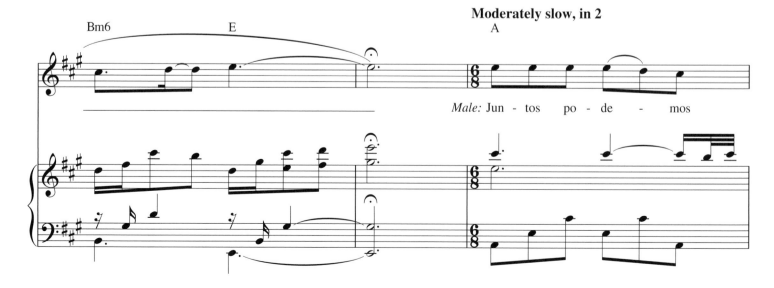

se - guir _____ Dar - le o - tro rum-ba a es - ta his - to - ria. _____
Female: Steal

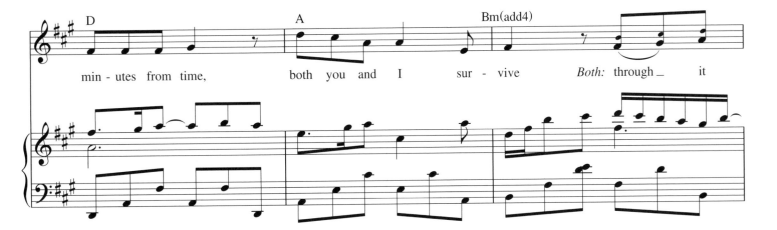

min - utes from time, both you and I sur - vive *Both:* through _ it

all. *Male:* Dí - me que _ pue - des sen - tir _____

Que no ter - mi - ne es - te sue - ño _____
Female: With the song and dance,

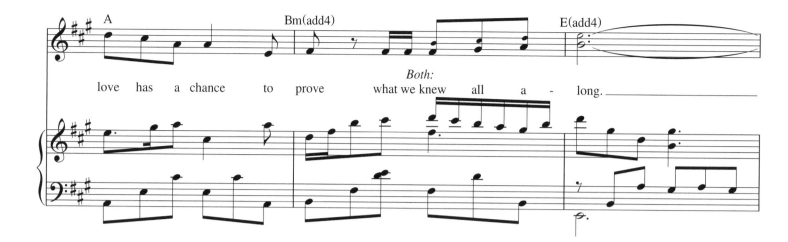

love has a chance to prove what we knew all a - long. _____

Both:

___ So - mos los dueñ - os del tiem - po

Bai - la con - mi - go en el vien - to Des - nu - da tus sen - ti -

mien - tos Has - ta el úl - ti - mo mo - men - to _____ Mi

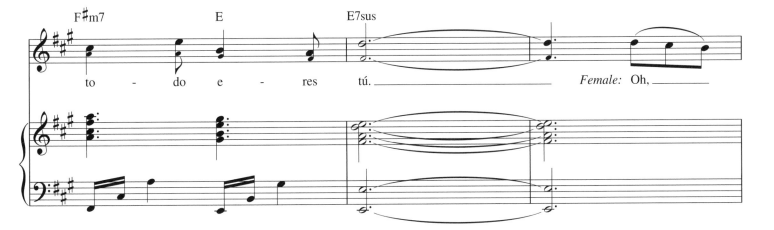

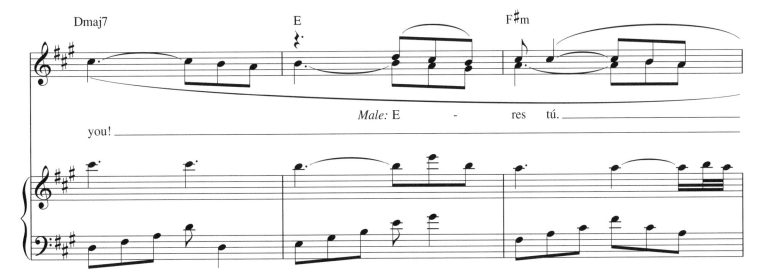

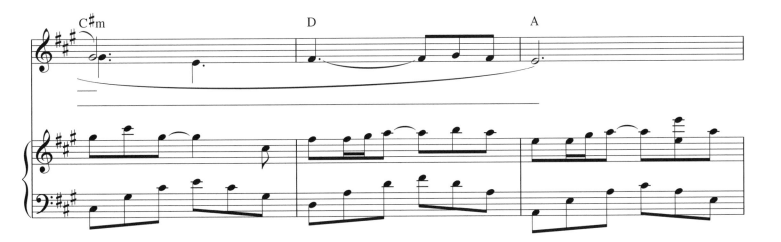

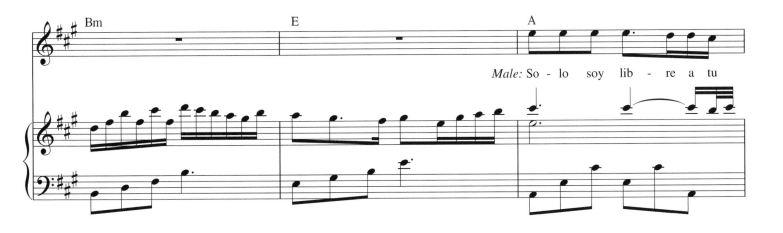

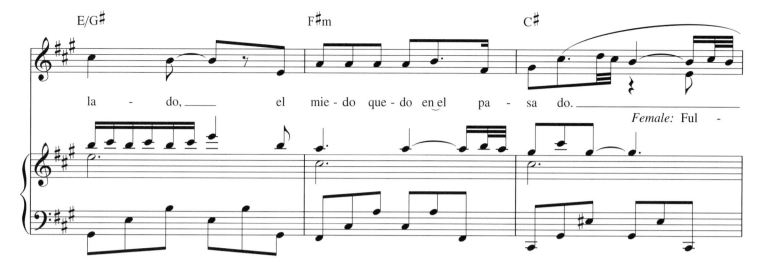

la - do, _____ el mie-do que-do en el pa - sa do. _____

Female: Ful -

fill me now with this end - less vow _____ to live

Both: as nev - er be -

fore. _____

So - mos los dueñ - os del

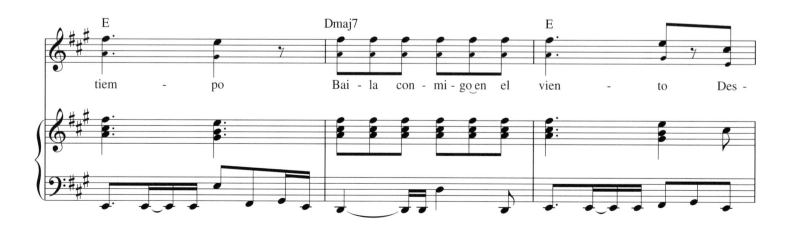

tiem - po

Bai - la con - mi-go en el vien - to

Des -

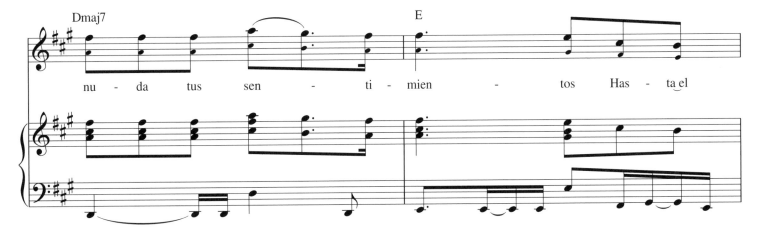

nu - da tus sen - ti - mien - tos Has - ta el

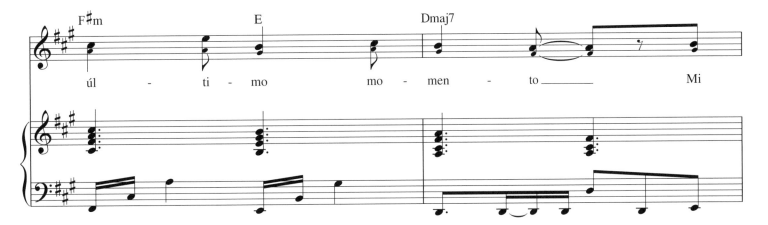

úl - ti - mo mo - men - to _____ Mi

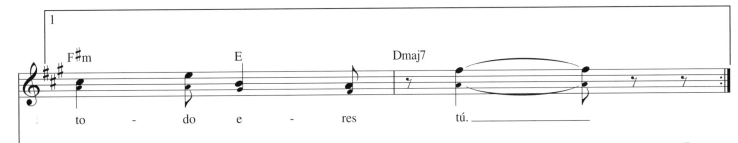

1

to - do e - res tú. _____

2

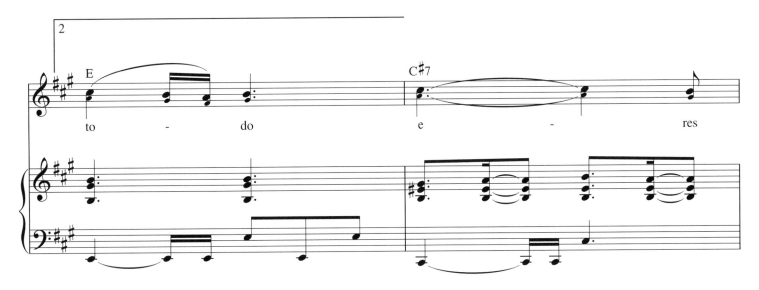

to - do e - res

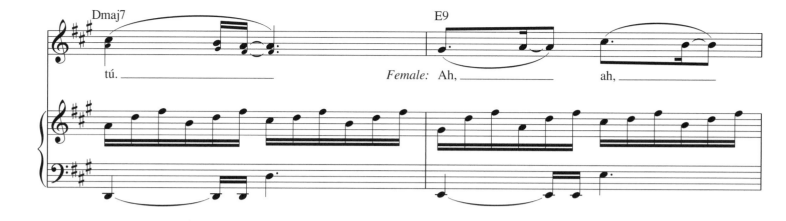

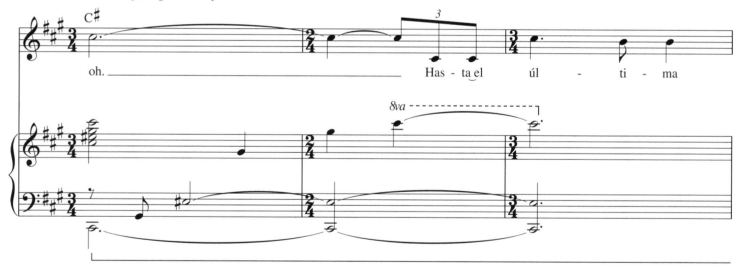

Moderately, expressively

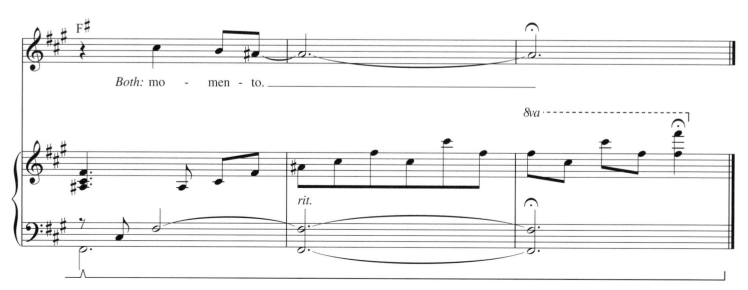

RITUAL DE AMOR

Music by YANNI
Lyrics by KARLA APONTE
Additional Music by CESAR LEMOS

Llen-a el ai - re con mis an-to - jos Pren-de el fue - go en mi_ co - ra-zón.
Rí - e, bai - la, suel-ta-te el pe - lo To-dos quier - en ver-te bai-lar

Que te a-cer - quen to - dos los o - jos. Que si_ te-mues-tra pa-sión. Bai-la-
Tu her-mo-su-ra en-cien-de los sue - ños Pro-vo-ca ga-nas de a-mar. Ne-ga-

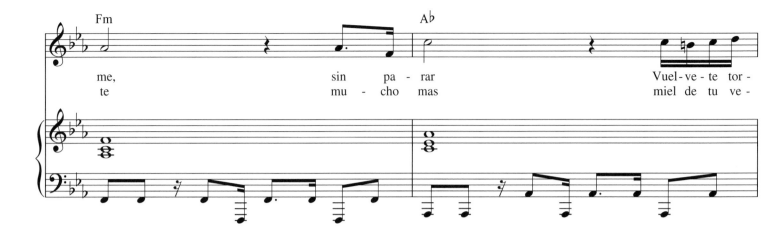

me,   sin pa - rar   Vuel - ve - te tor -
te   mu - cho mas   miel de tu ve -

men - ta en mi mar_____   Que te
ne - no me da._____   Ten - go

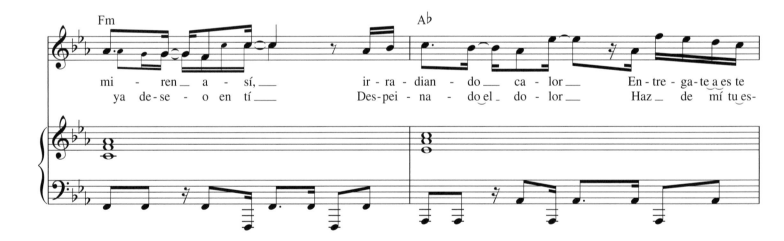

mi ren a - sí,___   ir - ra - dian - do_ ca - lor___   En - tre - ga - te a es te
ya de - se - o en tí___   Des - pei - na - do el_ do - lor___   Haz_ de mí tu es -

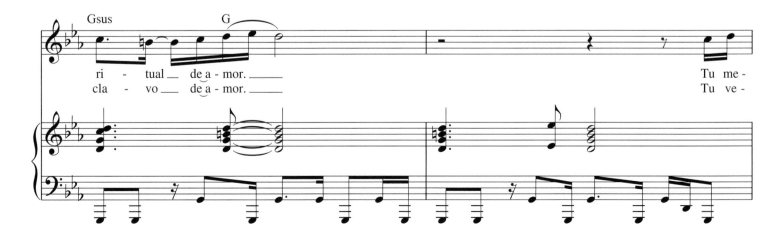

ri - tual _ de a - mor. ____   Tu me -
cla - vo___ de a - mor. ____   Tu ve -

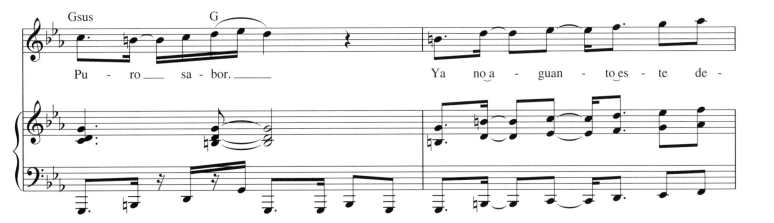

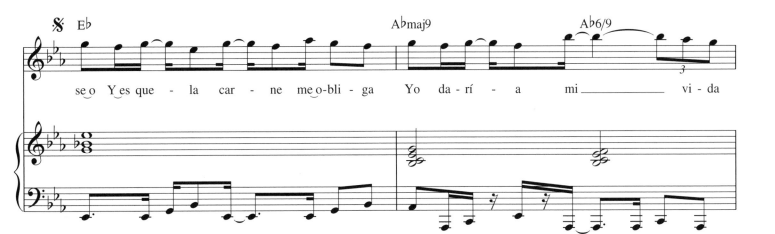

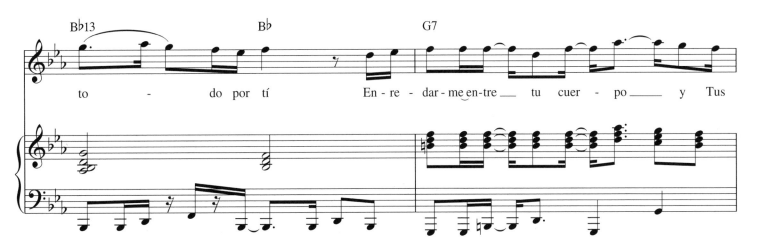

la - bios in - va - dir __ Tan si - quie - ra un __ mo - men - to _____ Ser - lo

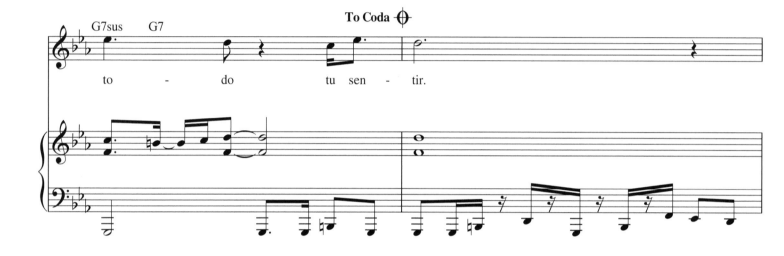

to - do tu sen - tir.

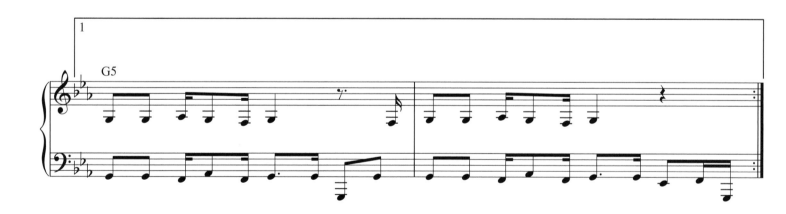

D.S. al Coda

Ya no a - guan - to es - te de -

CODA

ti. Tu ve - ne - no vuel - ve lo - co a cualquie - ra

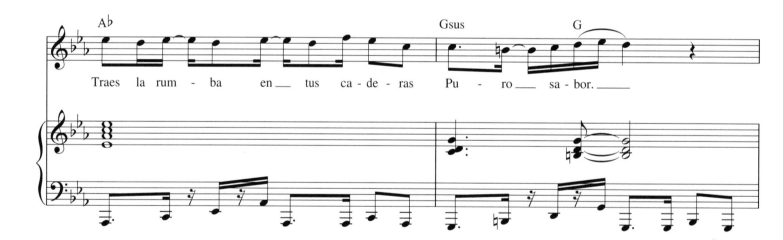

Traes la rum - ba en __ tus ca - de - ras Pu - ro __ sa - bor. ____

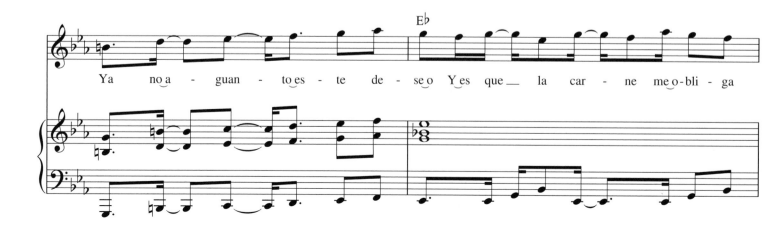

Ya no a - guan - to es - te de - se o Y es que __ la car - ne me o - bli - ga

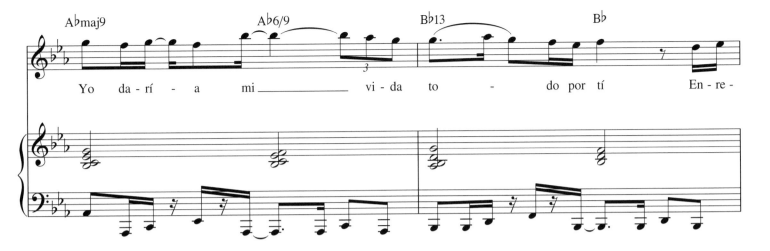

MOMENTS WITHOUT TIME

Written by YANNI
Additional Music by CESAR LEMOS

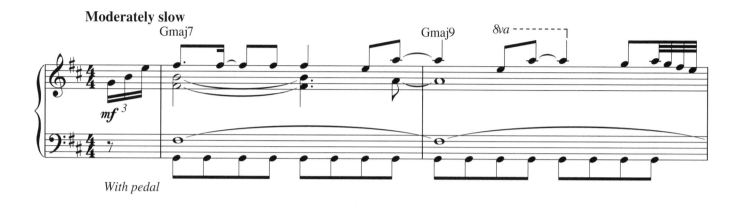

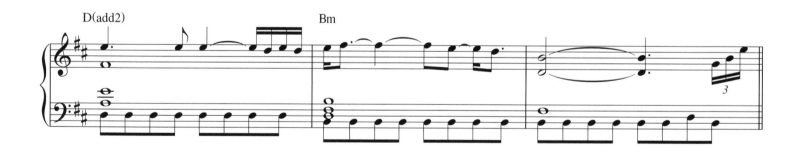

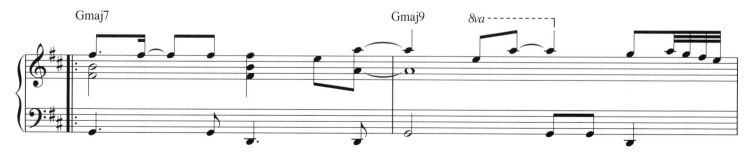

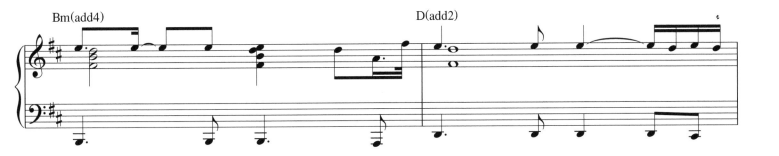

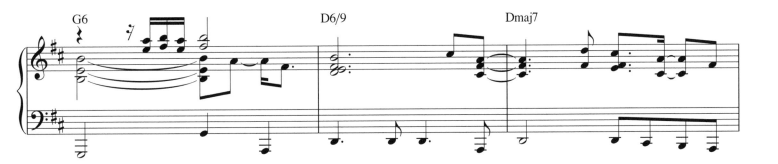

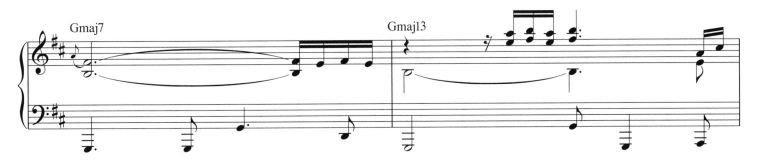

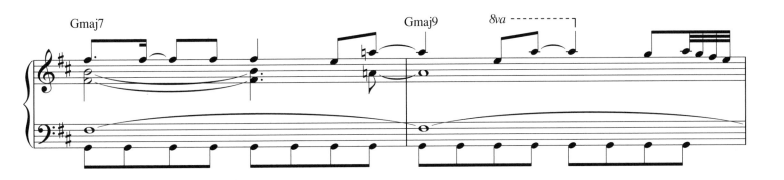

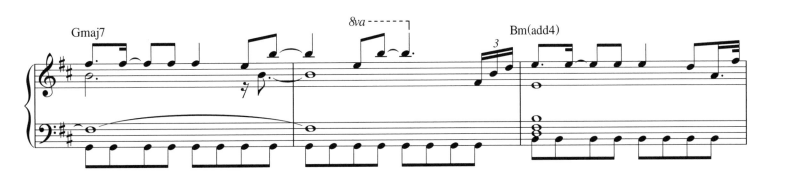

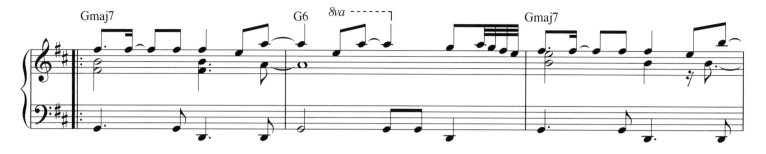

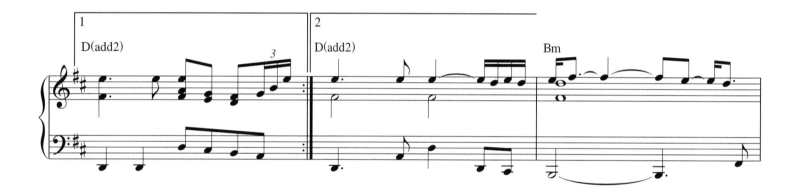

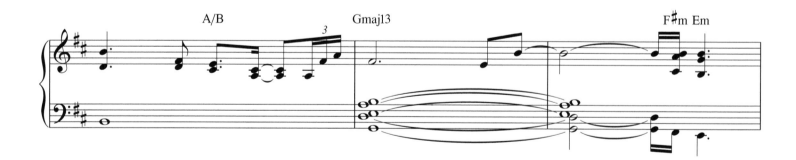

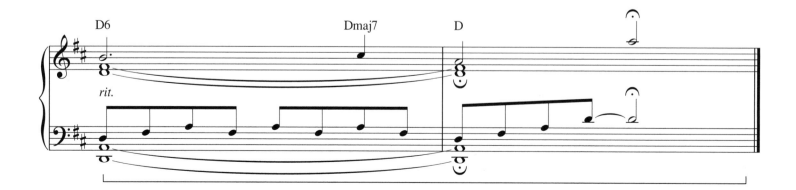

NEI TUOI OCCHI

Music by YANNI
Lyrics by NATHAN PACHECO and CHLOE LOWERY
Additional Music by CESAR LEMOS

Co - me u - cel - li - ni Li in - co - rag - gia vo -

lare. *Female:* In the mir - ror, our ___

love will ___ be _____ Through ___ the

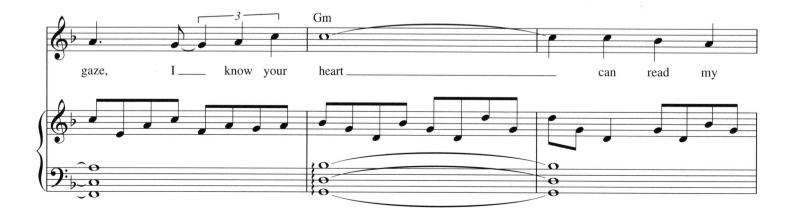

gaze, I ___ know your heart _____ can read my

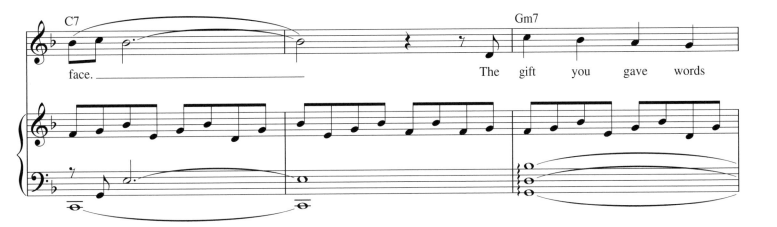

face. _____ The gift you gave words

can't re - pay, your eyes can on - ly say *Both:* Il tuo

sguar - do è __ la te - la ____ il mi - o

cie - lo Di - pin - to __ di stel - le __ bril -

lan - ti. _____ U - na bus - so - la ___ nei

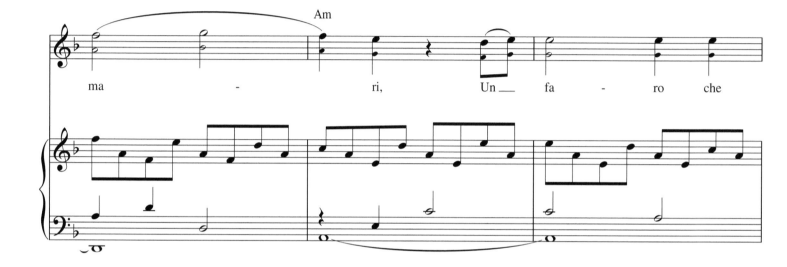

ma ___ - ri, Un ___ fa - ro che

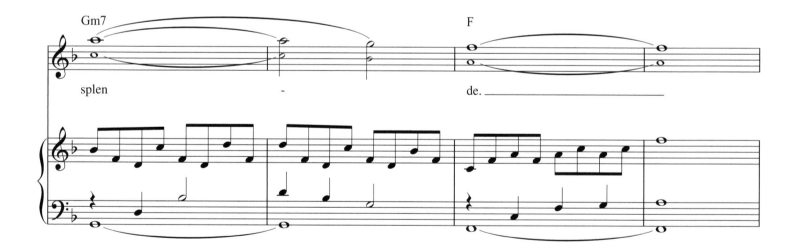

splen - de. _____

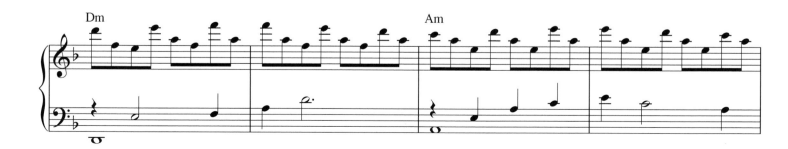

le. _____ *Both:* Mi dai cor - ag - gio _____ e a -

mo - re ____ Nel - le dif - fi - col - tà. Va - do

ver - so ____ il so - le ____ Se - guen - do ____ la

lu - ce Las - cian - do ____ il mi - o ____ pas -

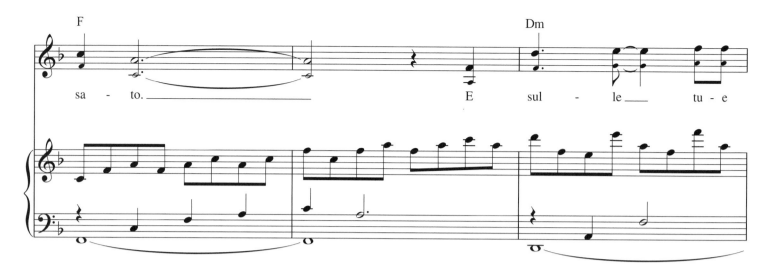

sa - to. _____

E sul - le ___ tu - e

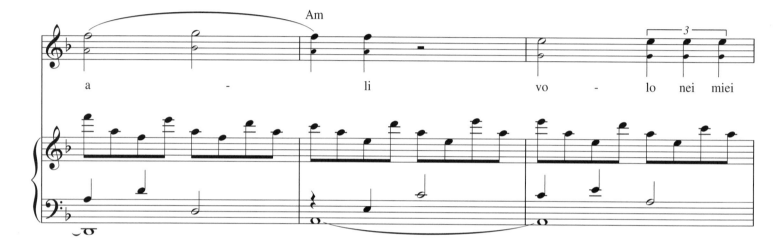

a - li

vo - lo nei miei

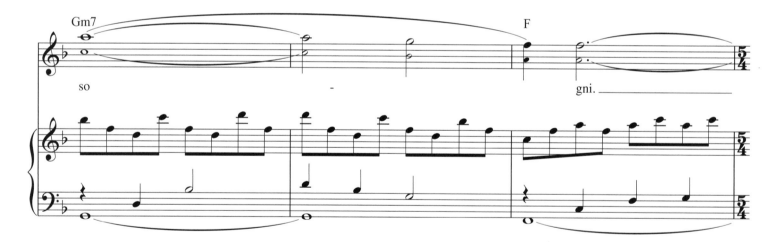

so -

gni. _____

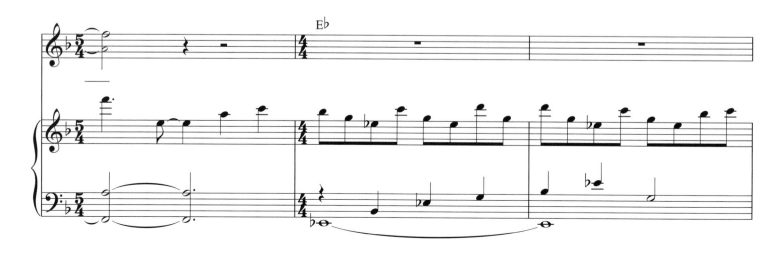

Male: Sem - pre Both: con

te.

rit.

Slower

Male: Tu co -

accel.

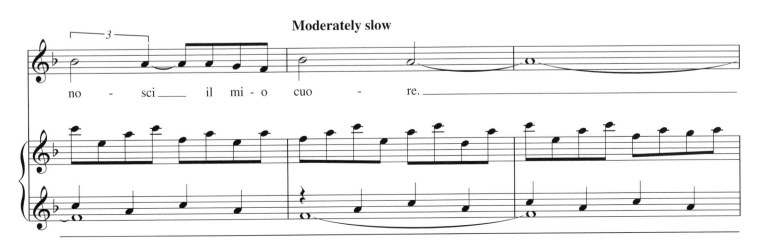

Moderately slow

no - sci il mi - o cuo - re.

Female: I'll hold it as you hold _____

_____ my dreams _____ in your hands. _____ *Male:* E

co - me bam - bi - ni Li in - cor - ag - gio a cam - mi -

nare. _____ *Female:* In the mir - ror _____ our _____

love will _____ be. _____ *Male:* I tuoi

Gm7

oc - chi ri - flet _____ to - no ve - ri -

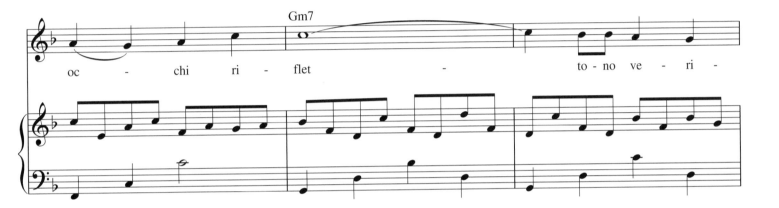

C7   Gm7

tà. _____ *Both:* E den - tro _____ ve - do

F

do - ve il _____ mio des - ti - no an - drà.   Il tuo

squar - do è __ la te - la _____ Il mi - o

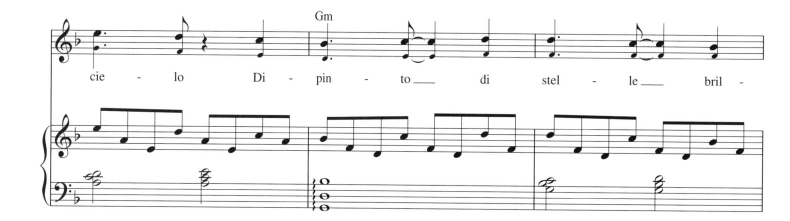

cie - lo Di - pin - to __ di stel - le __ bril -

lan - ti. _____ U - na bus - so - la __ nei

ma - ri Un fa - ro che

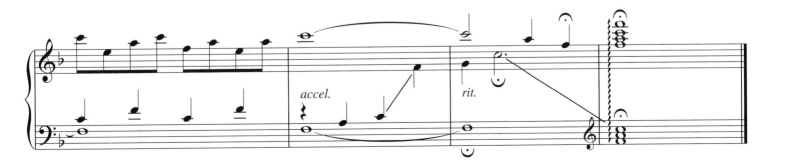

AMARE DI NUOVO

Music by YANNI
Lyrics by NATHAN PACHECO

Slowly in 1, expressively

Com' è dol - ce la pri - ma - ve - ra

do - po il fred - do in - ver - no. Sì, la ter - ra as - pet - ta il

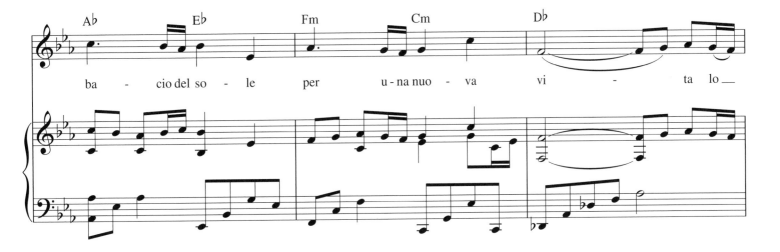

ba - cio del so - le per u - na nuo - va vi - ta lo__

sai. A - mo - re,__ tu__ sei il so - le, La

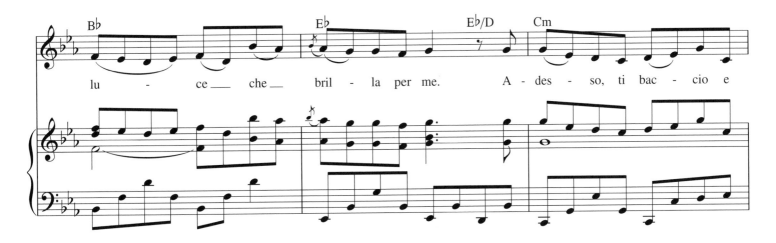

lu - ce__ che__ bril - la per me. A - des - so, ti bac - cio e

vi - vo A - mo - re, lo so che non c'è vi - ta sen - za te. Tu sei il

so - le, la lu - na, la stel - la più bel - la Il mi - o mon - do

gi - ra in - sie - me a te. Tu sei l'au - ro - ra, la lu - ce che

splen - de al mat - ti - no, Me - ra - vi - glio - sa me - lo -

di - a che suo - na per me.

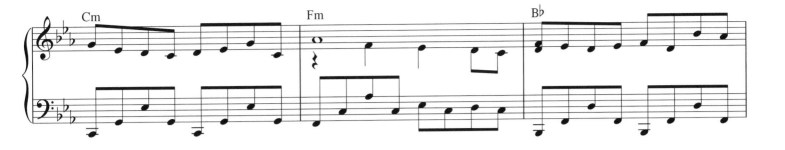

A - mo - re, vor - rei_____ spie - gar - ti, E non

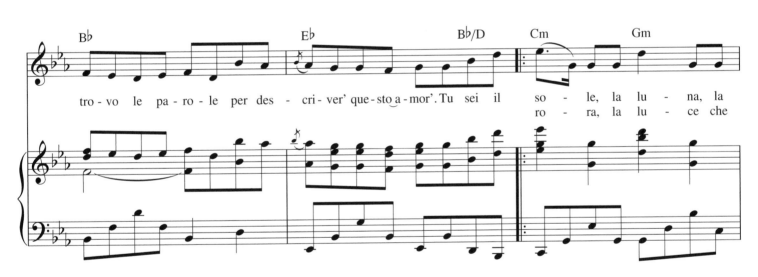

tro - vo le pa - ro - le per des - cri - ver' que-sto a - mor'. Tu sei il so - le, la lu - na, la

ro - ra, la lu - ce che

stel - la più bel - la Ed io ap-par-ten - go a te.

splen - de al mat - ti - no,___ Mer - a - vi-glio - sa

Tu sei l'au -

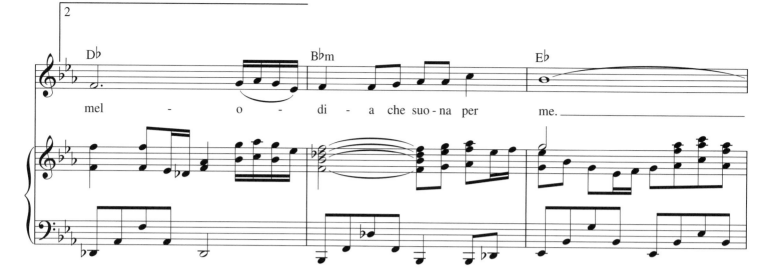

mel - o - di - a che suo-na per me.

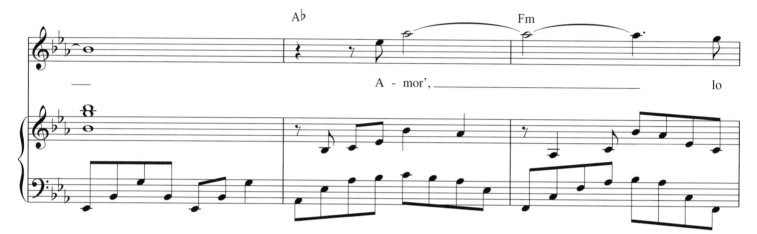

A - mor', lo

sai quan - to t'a - mo? A - mor',

dia - mo - ci la ma - no.

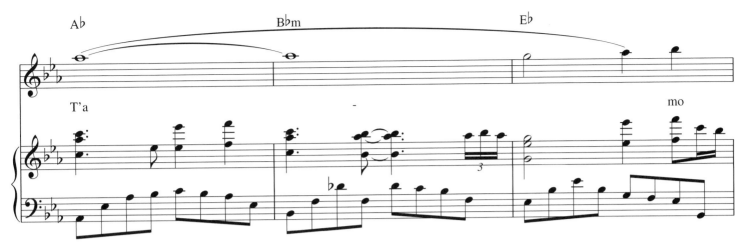

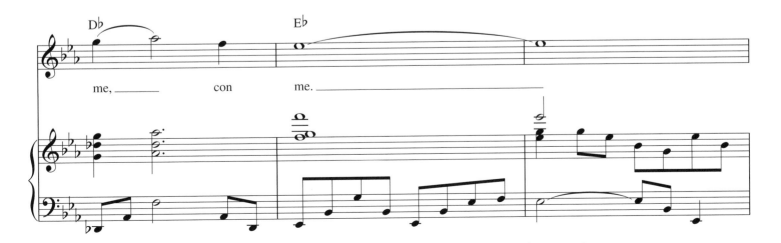

Lo so che sem-pre ti a - me - rò._____

Sem - pre ti a - me -

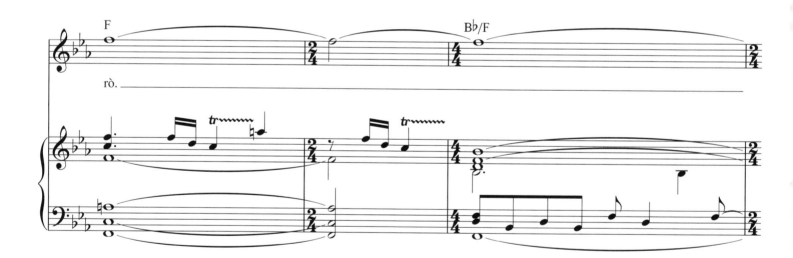

rò._____

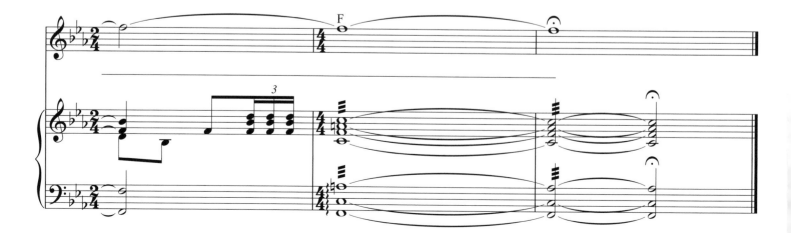